# The Internet

## A Curriculum Oriented Guide

By

Joanne J. Troutner

This book is a work of non-fiction. Names and places have been changed to protect the privacy of all individuals. The events and situations are true.



ISBN: 1-4107-5593-2 (e-book)
ISBN: 1-4107-5592-4 (Paperback)

This book is printed on acid free paper.

1stBooks - rev. 06/18/03

# Dedication

To my supportive and wonderful husband, Lary

## Acknowledgements

I would like to thank the educators of the Tippecanoe School Corporation, Lafayette, Indiana and the Minot Public School District, Minot, North Dakota for their help in shaping my educational philosophy and teaching skills.

## Table of Contents

# Basic Internet Information

Use this section to:

- ✓ Provide background for students and colleagues unfamiliar with the Internet or web browsers
- ✓ As a quick review at the start of the school year or grading period
- ✓ Level the playing field in a class of mixed abilities and Internet knowledge
- ✓ Provide a reminder that using the Print Preview feature is a good use of time
- ✓ Gather classroom management tips for use with technology projects

Joanne J. Troutner

# Netscape Information

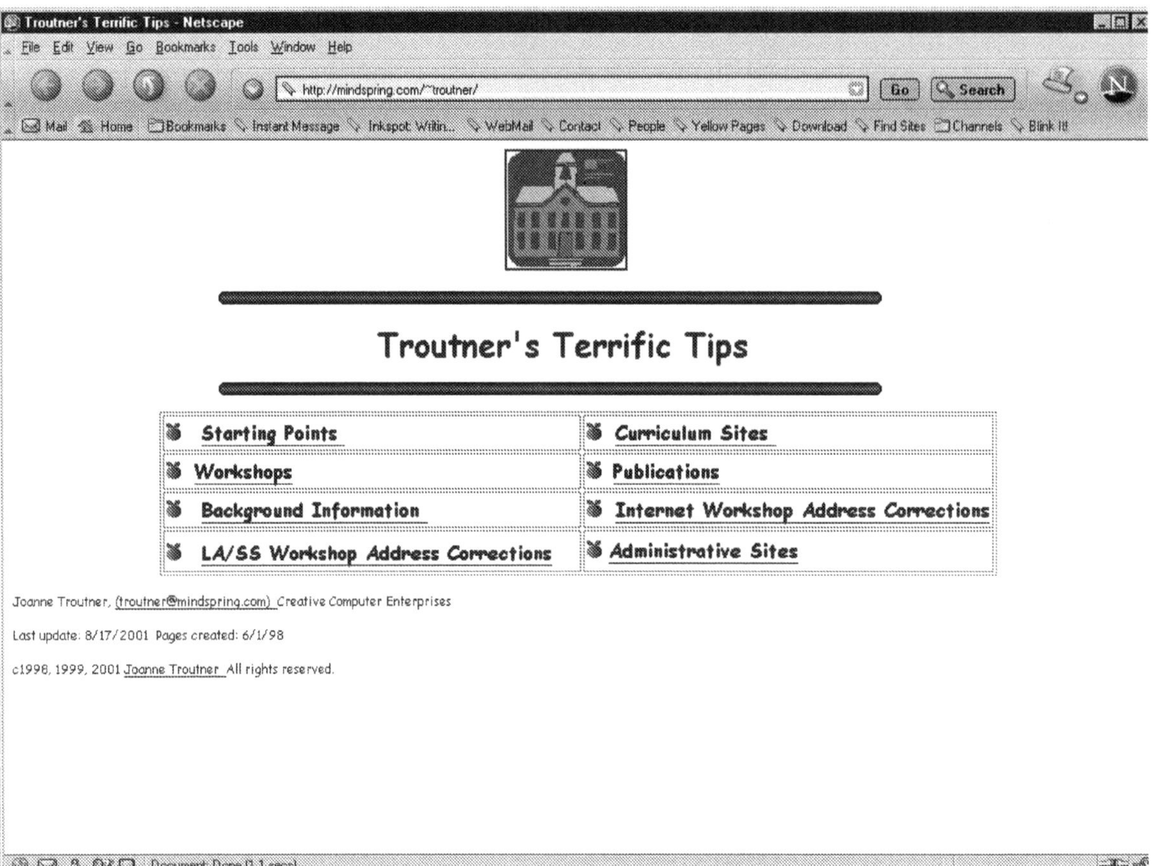


## Tool Bar Icons

| | |
|---|---|
| Back | Displays the previous page in the history list. A history list contains the pages you have viewed since you opened a Navigator window; when you close the window the history list is discarded. |
| | |
| Forward | Displays the next page in the history list |
| | |
| Home | Displays the home page set in the Netscape options |
| | |
| Reload | Redisplays the current page |
| | |
| Print | Displays the print dialog box and allows access to Print Preview |
| | |
| Stop | Halts any ongoing transfer of page information |
| | |
| Pointing Finger Icon | Displayed when text indicates another Internet link is available |

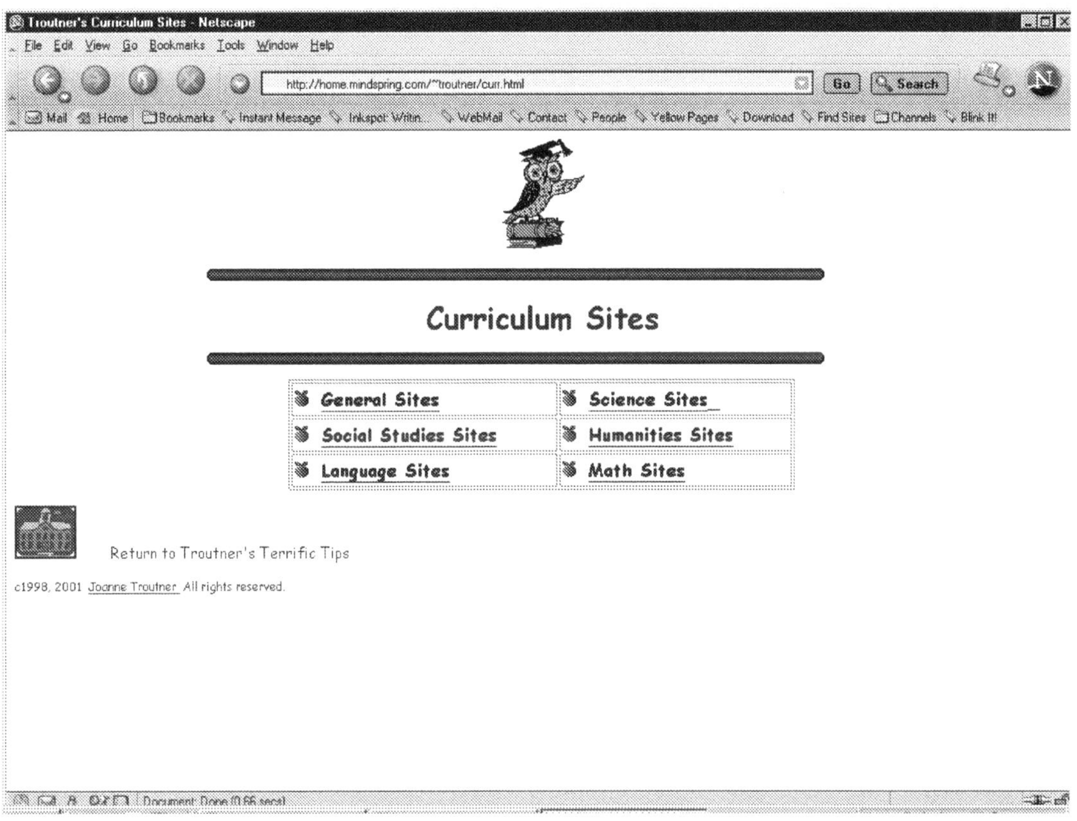


| Status Message Field | Bottom of Netscape screen. Displays amount loaded and when document is done. |
|---|---|
| | |
| Shortcuts | Bottom right of Netscape screen. Icons will take you directly to various parts of Netscape such as getting mail or composer. |
| | |
| Status Indicator | Upper right corner Netscape icon. Animated stars indicate a transfer is in progress. |
| | |
| Location Bar | Under the tool bar icons, shows the URL of the current page. Clicking the down arrow shows a series of sites previously visited. |
| | |
| Bookmarks | A list of frequently used pages. Select the Bookmarks menu and choose Add Bookmark. The list can be exported to disk and loaded into other computers. |
| | |
| History List | Click the Go menu, select History and choose from the list of sites you have visited in this session. |

Joanne J. Troutner

# Internet Explorer Information

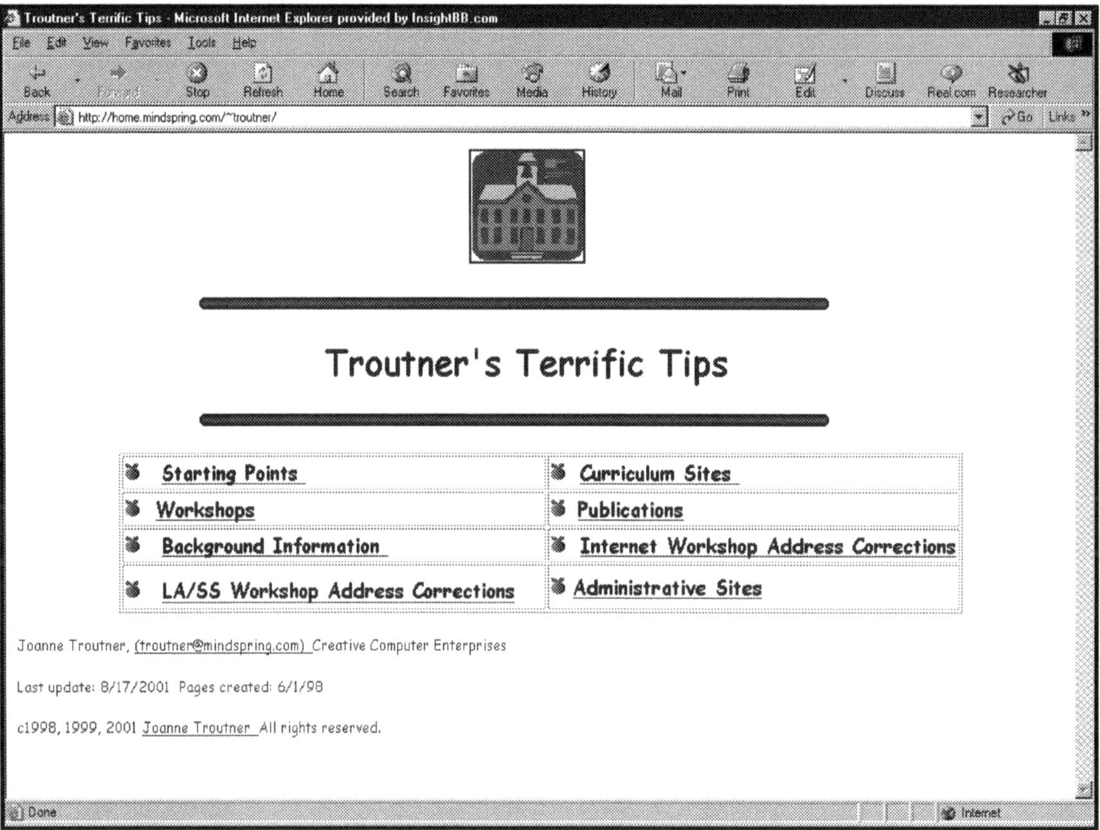


- **Tool Bar Icons**

| Back | Displays the previous page in the history list. A history list contains the pages you have viewed since you opened a Navigator window; when you close the window the history list is discarded. |
|---|---|
| | |
| Forward | Displays the next page in the history list |
| | |
| Home | Displays the home page set in the Netscape options |
| | |
| Refresh | Redisplays the current page |
| | |
| Search | Opens a search engine in a frame on the left side of the screen |
| | |
| Stop | Halts any ongoing transfer of page information |
| | |
| Favorites | Takes you to your list of favorite and often used sites |
| | |
| Print | Automatically prints the page. Use the File menu to access Print Preview and the Print dialog box. |

| History | Displays the sites that have been visited on this computer. Length of time for keeping the history can be set from the View menu under Internet Options.... |
|---|---|
| | |
| Mail | Takes you to a menu of e-mail options |
| | |
| Pointing Finger Icon | Displayed when text indicates another Internet link is available |

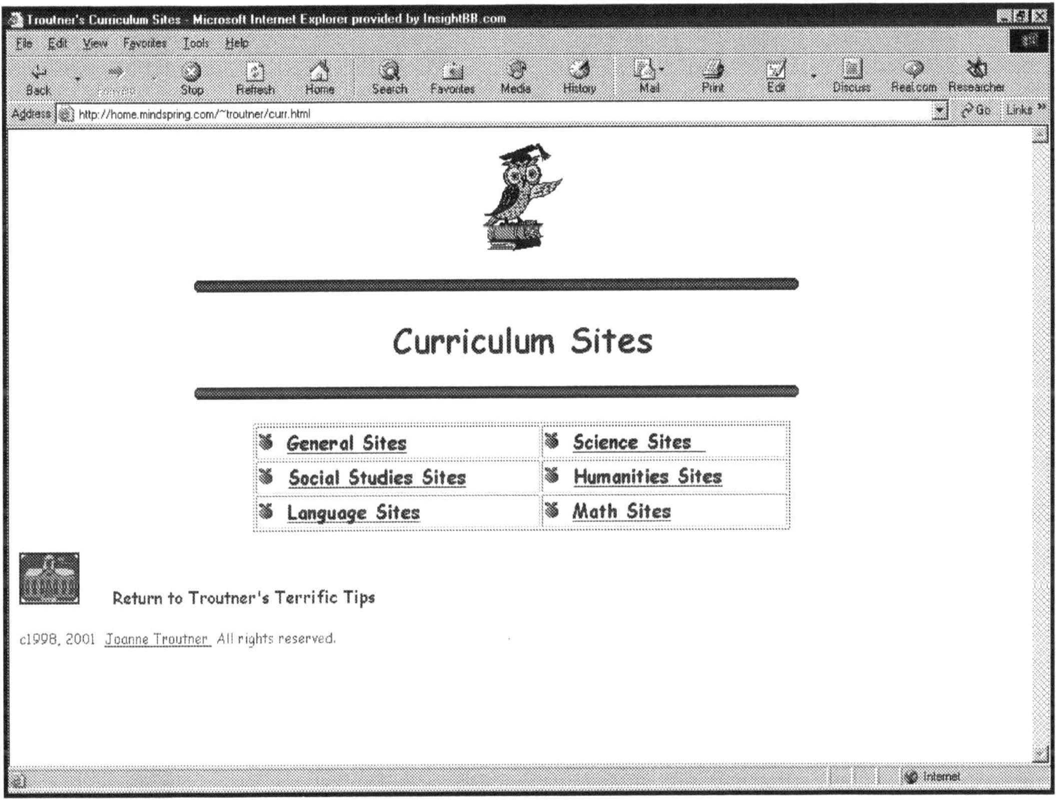


| Status Message Field | Bottom of Internet Explorer screen. Displays amount loaded and when document is done. |
|---|---|
| | |
| Status Indicator | Upper right corner Internet Explorer icon. Animated "e" indicates a transfer is in progress. |
| | |
| Address Bar | Under the tool bar icons, shows the URL of the current page. Clicking the down arrow shows a series of sites previously visited. |

# Using Print Preview

1. Pull down the File menu in either Netscape or Internet Explorer.

2. Select Print Preview.

3. You will see a screen similar to the following. There may be a short delay as the page loads.

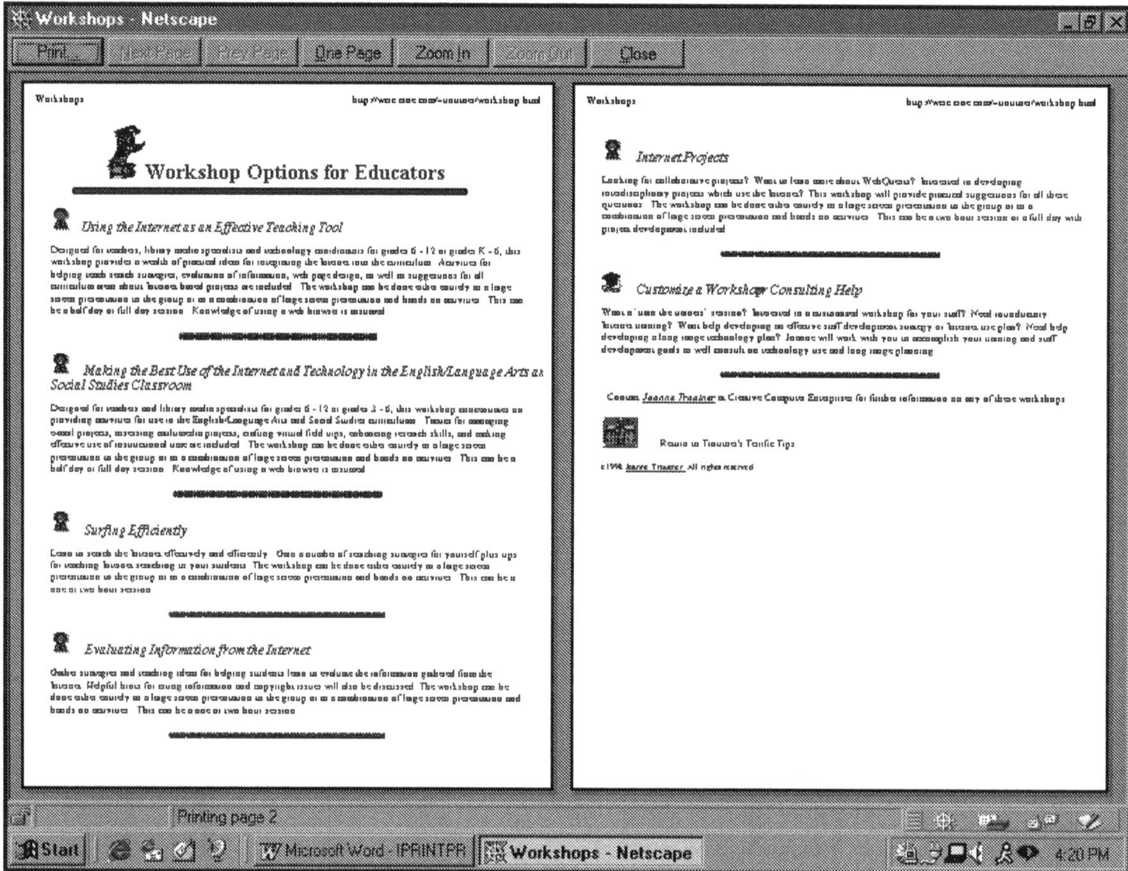


4. Use the Zoom In feature, if needed, to see more detail.

5. Determine what pages you want to print.

6. Select the Print button from the Print Preview screen.

7. Type in the page numbers you want printed in Page Range box.

# Saving Graphics

✓ ***Using Netscape***

1. Put the mouse cursor on the graphic and click the right hand mouse button. Hold down the mouse button until the menu appears on the Macintosh.

2. Select the *Save Image As* option.

3. You may change the file name of the graphic. Save the image with the suggested file format. This will usually be either gif or jpeg.

✓ ***Using Internet Explorer***

1. Put the mouse cursor on the graphic and click the right hand mouse button. Hold down the mouse button until the menu appears on the Macintosh.

2. Select the *Save Picture As* option.

3. You may change the file name of the graphic. Save the image with the suggested file format. This will usually be either gif or jpeg.

Public domain photo courtesy of U.S. Fish and Wildlife Service

Joanne J. Troutner

# Getting Graphics for Projects

***Digital Cameras*—**

These cameras store pictures on either diskettes, small CD's or memory cards in digital format. This means the images are easily transferred to the computer and student multimedia projects.

Questions to ask—

- What additional software is needed on the computer?
- What additional cables are needed to connect to the computer?
- How many pictures does the storage device hold?
- What do the storage devices cost?

***Scanners*—**

Scanners convert text and pictures to digital format for use with the computer and student multimedia projects.

Questions to ask—

- What additional software is needed on the computer?
- What additional cables are needed to connect to the computer?
- What additional cards are needed in the computer?

## Pictures from the Internet—

It is very easy to save most graphics and pictures found on web pages.

Simply put the mouse cursor on the picture or graphic you wish to save, click the right mouse button if on a Windows machine or hold down the mouse button if on a Macintosh. A menu appears. Select "Save Image As…" and store the image at whatever location you wish.

However, this practice provides a wealth of copyright violations.

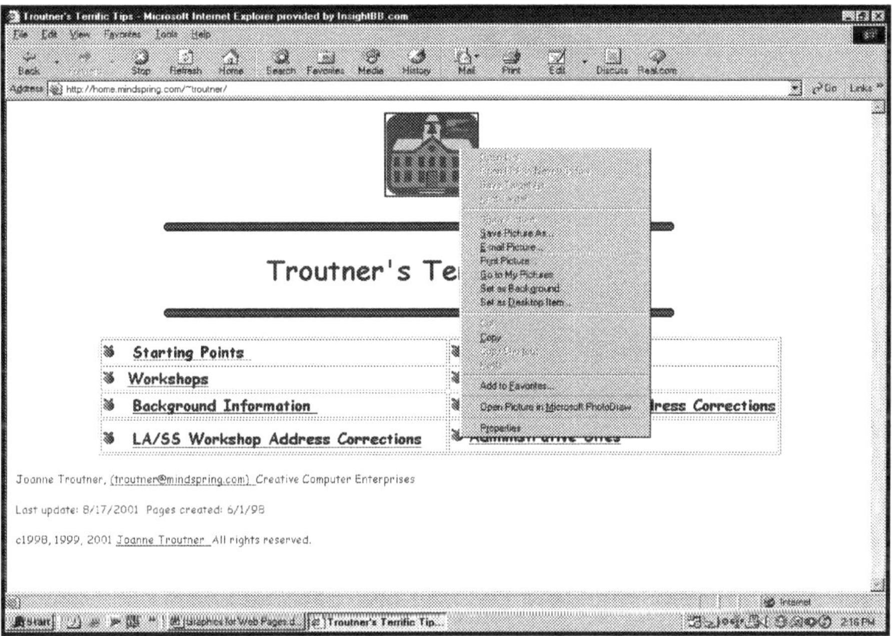


Another option is to visit a number of clip art web sites, which provide either free or shareware graphics for use in student projects.

| | |
|---|---|
| ✂ Discovery School's Clip Art Gallery | //school.discovery.com/clipart/ |
| ✂ Google Image Finder | //www.google.com |
| ✂ Image Finder | //sunsite.berkeley.edu/ImageFinder/ |
| ✂ Kids Click—Image Search | //www.kidsclick.org/psearch.html |
| ✂ The Amazing Picture Machine | //www.ncrtec.org/picture.htm |
| ✂ Copyright-Friendly Images for Education | //pics.tech4learning.com/ |

---

Be aware that you can easily import text directly from the Internet into a word processor. Plagiarism has become even easier for students! OR, you can teach this as a time saving way to take notes.

1. In your web browser, highlight the text you wish to import.
2. Pull down the *Edit* menu.
3. Select *Copy.*
4. Open your word processing program.
5. Start a new file.
6. Place the cursor where you want to import the text.
7. Click on the paste button from the tool bar.

> Be sure to read Jamie McKenzie's article on ***The New Plagiarism*** at his web site, http://www.fno.org/may98/cov98may.html

# Managing Bookmarks or Favorites

✓ **Using Netscape**

Netscape stores web addresses you select in a section called Bookmarks.

***Adding a Bookmark***

1. Simply have the web page you wish to bookmark active in the browser window.
2. Click on the *Bookmarks* menu.
3. Click on *Bookmark This Page.*

***Putting Bookmarks in Folders***

1. Click on the *Bookmarks* menu.
2. Select *File Bookmarks.*
3. Select the appropriate folder to *Create In* OR create a *New Folder.*

Work through the ***Effective Bookmarks Management*** tutorial done by the library at the University of California, Berkeley, //www.infopeople.org/howto/exercises/ Ex_bkmk_management.pdf

### ✓ Using Internet Explorer

Internet Explorer stores web addresses you select in a section called Favorites.

***Adding a Favorite***

1. Have the web page you wish to add as a Favorite active in the browser window.

2. Pull down the *Favorites* menu.

3. Select *Add Favorite.*

4. Answer the appropriate questions.

***Organizing Favorites***

1. Pull down the *Favorites* menu.

2. Select *Organize Favorites.*

3. Click on the *Favorite* you wish to organize.

4. Use the buttons at the bottom of the dialog box to move, change, or create a new folder for the Favorite.

> Use the ***IE Favorites Exercise*** link at
> //www.infopeople.org/howto/exercises/Ex_fave_management.pdf

# Understanding URL's or WWW Addresses

⇒ Sample Address http://www.ncrel.org/sdrs/pathwayg.htm

| | |
|---|---|
| ♦ http:// | is the start of any World Wide Web address |
| ♦ www.ncrel.org | says the information is found on a World Wide Web computer named ncrel and the ncrel is an organization domain |
| ♦ /sdrs/ | says the information resides in a folder named sdrs on the computer ncrel |
| ♦ pathwayg | is the specific file name of a webpage in the folder sdrs |
| ♦ .htm | tells that the information is written in HTML or hypertext markup language is readable by a web browser |

**Domain Names**

| | |
|---|---|
| ♦ com | commercial |
| ♦ edu | higher education |
| ♦ k12 | K - 12 education |
| ♦ gov | government |
| ♦ mil | military |
| ♦ net | network |
| ♦ org | organizations that are not commercial or educational |
| ♦ au | Australia |
| ♦ jp | Japan |
| ♦ uk | United Kingdom |
| ♦ other countries | Check the list at http://www.norid.no/domenenavnbaser/ domreg.html |

Joanne J. Troutner

# Rate Your Technology Ability

⇒ Use this chart to rate your Internet ability and that of your class.

### *Technology Knowledge*

| I'm an expert. I know the Internet and have been using it at home. I know how to use most tool software. | I'm comfortable with the computer as a tool for me, i.e. using word processing, etc. I have limited experience with the Internet. | I don't know anything about technology and the Internet scares me to death! |
|---|---|---|
| 5 | 3 | 1 |

### *Classroom Management*

| A SUPER group of students | An OK class | The class from #@#@#@$$!! |
|---|---|---|
| 5 | 3 | 1 |

### *Teacher-Based Learning vs. Student-Based Learning*

| Student directed learning for these students! | An even break between students who can direct their learning and those who need to be directed | Teacher directed learning is a must for these students |
|---|---|---|
| 5 | 3 | 1 |

Notice that only 1/3 of the equation is your individual technology knowledge! Be aware that using technology with teacher directed students is a workable but hard working experience.

# Acceptable Use Policy (AUP)

*Why does your school district need an AUP?*

Is it because...

⇒ every source you read says you need one?

⇒ your superintendent or principal asked you to write one?

⇒ you feel uneasy about allowing students access to Internet?

⇒ you know that an incident of having students find pornography on a school computer could kill telecommunications use in your district?

⇒ your governmental department of education has mandated that each school district have one?

⇒ you feel you need a written policy to protect the information rights of students?

⇒ to protect you as the classroom teacher?

The following sites on the Internet provide some excellent information and sample policies as you begin to tackle this issue for your classroom and/or district.

| | |
|---|---|
| • Bellingham Public Schools excellent examples of board approved policies | //www.bham.wednet.edu/ technology/techpolicies.htm |
| • *From Now On*, an electronic educational journal/look in back issues for Internet Use Policies | //www.fno.org/fnoindex.html - Internet |
| • The Internet Advocate | //www.monroe.lib.in.us/~lchampel/ netadv.html |

Joanne J. Troutner

# Classroom Management Tips

- Assign computers as you assign seats in the classroom. This makes it easier to check role and if there is any mischief it maybe easier to determine offender. This practice also saves time by allowing students to go directly to a computer and automatically logon.

- Some students have a hard time remembering their passwords and/or login names. Keep a record of login names and passwords for students. There are two ways to do this. Put them on index cards so students can take the card back to their computer. Also, have a master list for yourself.

- When leaving the computer lab make sure students log all the way off of the computer and they take with them any materials they brought with them.

- Implement a discipline procedure and enforce it.

- No food or drinks in lab.

- Make sure students are in correct programs.

- Only send one print command and if it does not print ask teacher.

- Use an assessment tool with a student performance component.

- Provide students with easy access to a list of targeted sites. This can be a Word document with links to the sites, a distributed list of bookmarks, or shortcuts to the web sites.

- Make effective use of off-line activities. Have the students plan projects on paper prior to beginning work on the computer.

- Decide on a method of handling student questions. For example, the student asks at least two other people before asking the teacher or provide cups for placing on top of the monitor when student has a question.

- Take time to introduce the activity to the entire class with a projection device.

# Research Strategies & Tips

Use this section to:

- ✓ Gather ideas for crafting research projects
- ✓ Gain quick tips on helping prevent plagarism
- ✓ Provide Internet searching strategies for your students
- ✓ Gather ideas for teaching information evaluation skills

Joanne J. Troutner

# Crafting Research Assignments

### Types of Questions to Ask—

- ✓ Why does something happen as it does? This is the basic tool for constructivist learning.
- ✓ How could something be made better? This is the basic tool for problem solving and synthesis.
- ✓ Which something will I choose? This is the basic tool for thoughtful decision making.

### Level I Assignments—

- ✓ Tell me just the facts about Lincoln, a Civil War battle, the US involvement in Korea, the life of Gandhi.
- ✓ Tell me just the facts about Shakespeare, the life of Edgar Allan Poe, the history of literature in Great Britain during the Middle Ages.

### Level II Assignments—

- ✓ Tell me other people's ideas about why the South lost the Civil War, the success of the New Deal, the success of Lewis and Clark, the current status of NATO, the writings of Robert Frost, the success of Mark Twain as a writer.

### Level III Assignments—

- ✓ Tell me in your humble opinion—

  How do we restore peace in the Middle East?<br>
  Why didn't the South win the Civil War?<br>
  What city or country would make the best host for the Olympics?<br>
  Which world leaders should be in the Top Five Hall of Fame?<br>
  What are the advantages and disadvantages of having power?<br>
  How does the power of press influence decision making?<br>
  Which authors should be on the Top Five list for American literature?

Take time to read this article by Jamie McKenzie—
The New Plagiarism at //fno.org/may98/cov98may.html

# A Toolkit for Questions

**Essential Questions—**

- ✓ Provide the organizing focus for a unit
- ✓ Deal with issues such as leadership, courage, purpose, identity, honor, integrity, invention
- ✓ Are interdisciplinary in nature
- ✓ Are at the top of Bloom's taxonomy—analyze, evaluate, synthesize

**Subsidiary Questions—**

- ✓ The smaller questions which much be answered before the essential question
- ✓ Use a graphic organizer to group the subsidiary questions

**Hypothetical Questions—**

- ✓ Useful when trying to solve a problem
- ✓ "What would happen if" type of questions

**Telling Questions—**

- ✓ Very focused, find evidence and information
- ✓ Instead of "Which would be the best company to invest in—Disney or Coke?"—"Which company has the best dividend returns for the past five years?"

Take time to read Jamie McKenzie's article, "A Questioning Toolkit at //fno.org/nov97/toolkit.html

Think about your next teaching unit. What are the essential questions or the "take home" messages?

# Research Organizer

Fill out items 1 – 5 **before you begin** work on your project.

## Define the Task

Answer the question, “What am I supposed to do?”.

## Strategies for Finding Information

What are the possible places/sources to find this information?

Which of the above are the best ones for this project?

## Location of the Resources

Where will I find the sources I have chosen?

Who can help me find information?

## Use of the Information

How will I record the information I find?

How will I cite the sources I use?

## Synthesis

What product or performance will I make to finish this project? Visualize the results of your work and describe it.

How will I cite my sources in my final product or performance?

## Evaluation

How will I know I have done my personal best on this project?

Did I select the best resources for finding the information I needed?

Did I use the best methods to locate the information?

This organizer is based on a research process called "The Big Six." To learn more about this process check out the Big Six web site at //www.big6.com/

# Citing Electronic Information

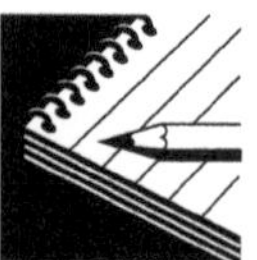

Students need to be sure to cite information sources. This is a practice often overlooked when developing multimedia projects. Please be sure your students learn about copyright and citing electronic information. Consider the following examples and use the web sites to help you teach this concept to your students.

World Wide Web based on APA style.

Troutner, Joanne J. (1998, June 16). *Troutner's Terrific Tips*. [Online]. Lafayette, IN: Author. Available: http://home.mindspring.com/~troutner/index.html [2003, March 28].

World Wide Web based on MLA style.

Troutner, Joanne J. *Troutner's Terrific Tips*. 16 June, 1998. http://home.mindspring.com/~troutner/index.html. Accessed 28 March 28, 2003.

| | |
|---|---|
| Citing Electronic Sources | //owl.english.purdue.edu/handouts/research/r_docelectric.html |
| | |
| Citing Electronic Resources | //www.westwords.com/guffey/ apa.html |

Look at Jamie McKenzie's electronic newsletter article on copyright and web site management. Many of the issues discussed pertain to student created projects and provide excellent starter activities for a quick lesson on copyright. This, of course, leads to the reminder to cite information!!!!

*Keeping it Legal: Questions Arising out of Web Site Management,* //www.fno.org/jun96/legal.html

Also check out this well developed link on copyright information—*Before You Post Your Work,* //www.ncsu.edu/midlink/posting.html

# Taking Notes with a Database

- Use any database such as AppleWorks, Microsoft Works for Windows, Star Office or another software you like.

- Create fields for the following information:

  - ✓ Source
  - ✓ Subject Words
  - ✓ Key Words or Subheadings
  - ✓ Abstract/Notes

- Keep your notes in this electronic form for this project. See the example below, which is a data view printout from Microsoft Works.

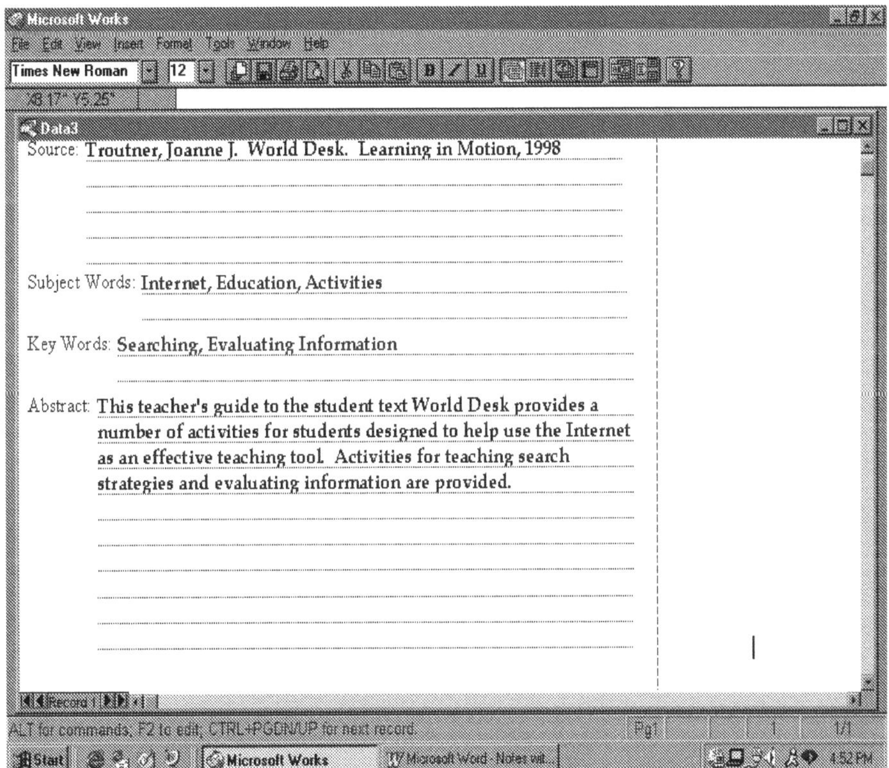

Joanne J. Troutner

# Introducing Searching To Your Students

Begin by having the students learn to read search engine results. Provide two examples and compare the search engine results on paper. Look at the example searches on Shakespeare's Globe Theatre using Google and Alta Vista. Use the Search Engine Comparison graphic organizer. Have students work in pairs to complete the organizer.

I would suggest using Yahooligans and Ask Jeeves for Kids with upper elementary and middle school students. I would use Google and Alta Vista with high school students and Metacrawler and DogPile with AP students.

Next work with students on brainstorming search terms. Dig out that paper thesaurus, or use the thesaurus in Word or another word processor, or use the online Visual Thesaurus at http://www.visualthesaurus.com/index.jsp. Use the Which Search Terms to Use organizer.

When students are ready to start a research project, take 10 minutes to do a class search as a group with a projection device. This will save time in the long run as students gain an understanding of the search engine you will suggest they use. Also take time to brainstorm the search terms related to the topics.

Another time saving hint is to have students do their Internet searches and then move to a desk. Have the students circle the first 5 to 7 sites they think will be the best sources of information. Then allow the students to move back to the computer to visit these sites.

## *Sources of Information on Searching and Doing Research*

| | |
|---|---|
| 🕮 Spider's Apprentice | //www.monash.com/spidap.html |
| 🕮 Sink or Swim | //www.sci.ouc.bc.ca/libr/connect96/search.htm |
| 🕮 PBS Internet Info | //www.pbs.org/uti/ |
| 🕮 Searching for the Grail | //www.fno.org/jan98/searching.html |

# Search Hints & Tips

⇒ Try searching for the plural form of a word or using the "*" as a truncation symbol.

⇒ Try at least two search engines.

⇒ Try putting phrases in quotes. For instance "multiple intelligence" or "midwest weather".

⇒ Try using a hyphen to exclude a term. For instance "virtual tour" –Egypt or "virtual tour" -Africa.

⇒ Try using a + if the word must be included. For instance "virtual tour" + Gettysburg.

⇒ Be aware that not all search engines will make use of the quotes, hyphen, and plus signs.

| | | |
|---|---|---|
| ➢ Google | Advanced search options, caches web pages from results, has filtering option, searches images as well as PDF, PowerPoint, Word and other file types | //www.google.com/ |
| ➢ Lycos | Limited advanced search option, password protected filtering option | //www.lycos.com/ |
| ➢ InfoMine | Librarian selected searchable database of 23,000+ sites | //infomine.ucr.edu/ |
| ➢ Yahoo | Good help feature, advanced search options | //www.yahoo.com/ |
| ➢ Alta Vista | Good advanced search tutorial, password protected filtering option, search for images and audio separately | //www.altavista.com/ |
| ➢ Ask Jeeves | Allows natural language questions, includes sponsored sites, and metasearch engine results | //www.ask.com/ |

| | | |
|---|---|---|
| ➢ Hot Bot | Advanced search options, search for images, videos, and audio separately, good help feature | //www.hotbot.lycos.com/ |
| ➢ Fast | Simple user interface, advanced search options | //www.alltheweb.com/ |
| ➢ Britannica | Natural language option, initial search Britannica site only | //www.britannica.com/ |
| ➢ Yahooligans | Limited database for middle school students, filtered by virtue of small database | //www.yahooligans.com/ |
| ➢ Ask Jeeves for Kids | Upper elementary and middle school version of Ask Jeeves. Sites are selected by editors for content and "safe" sites | //www.ajkids.com/ |
| ➢ MetaCrawler | Use up to 13 search engines, good help feature and links to searching tutorials, collates hits | //www.metacrawler.com/ |
| ➢ Vivisimo | Compiles results and categories hits into folders on left side of screen | //vivisimo.com/ |
| ➢ Mamma | Searches top single search engines, collates hits, includes summary, can e-mail results | //www.mamma.com/ |
| ➢ ProFusion | Allows user selection of search engines, search type, number of hits, and checks links; collates hits; includes summary | //www.profusion.com/ |
| ➢ DogPile | Allows user to select search engines, hits not collated | //www.dogpile.com/ |
| ➢ Monster Crawler | Clean interface, compiled results, family friendly option | //www.monstercrawler.com/ |
| ➢ Beaucoup | Meta search option, contains best list of search engines by categories | //www.beaucoup.com |
| ➢ Tile.Net | Allows searching for listservs | //www.tile.net/ |

# Which Search Engine to Use

| | |
|---|---|
| ➢ Narrow a broad topic | Yahoo or any engine with directories, Vivisimo, Infomine |
| ➢ Small number of relevant hints | Metacrawler, Britannica |
| ➢ What's available on the Internet for my topic? | MetaCrawler, ProFusion, DogPile, Mamma |
| ➢ Quality, evaluated sites | Britannica |
| ➢ Pinpoint search | AltaVista |
| ➢ Date of an event | HotBot |
| ➢ Media type | HotBot, Alta Vista, Google |
| ➢ Scientific information | AltaVista |
| ➢ Geographic region | Metacrawler |
| ➢ Internet domain | Hot Bot, Google |
| ➢ Describe my topic in a sentence | Ask Jeeves |
| ➢ Biographical Information | Biography.com, Lives (http://amillionlives.com/), Biographical Dictionary (http://www.s9.com/biography/) |
| ➢ Quotations | Bartlett (http://www.bartleby.com/100/), Quoteland (http://www.quoteland.com/) |

# Google Search (www.google.com)

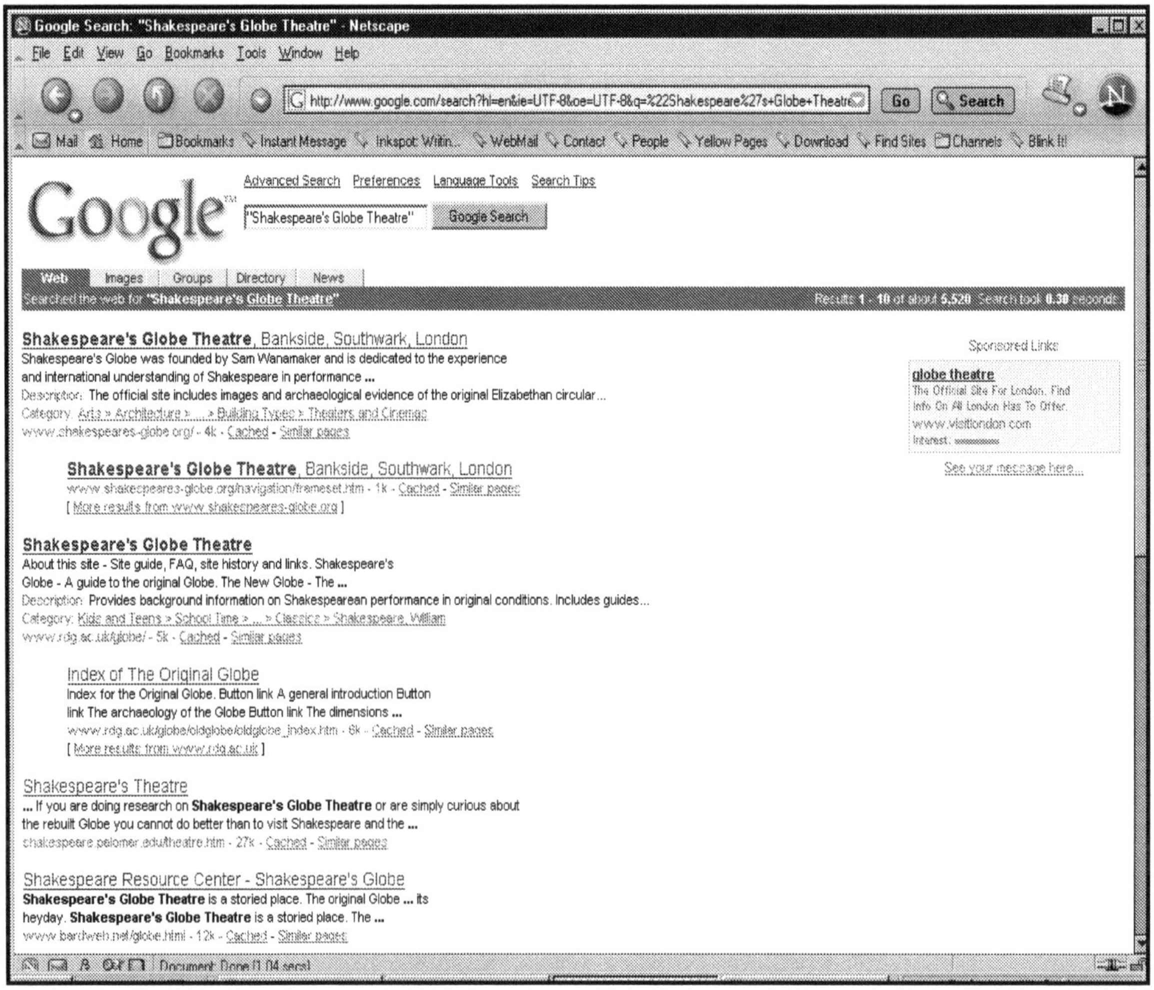

Google Search: "Shakespeare's Globe Theatre" - Netscape

File Edit View Go Bookmarks Tools Window Help

http://www.google.com/search?hl=en&ie=UTF-8&oe=UTF-8&q=%22Shakespeare%27s+Globe+Theatre

Go Search

Mail Home Bookmarks Instant Message Inkspot Writin... WebMail Contact People Yellow Pages Download Find Sites Channels Blink It!

Google™ Advanced Search Preferences Language Tools Search Tips

"Shakespeare's Globe Theatre" Google Search

Web Images Groups Directory News

Searched the web for **"Shakespeare's Globe Theatre"** Results **1** - **10** of about **5,520**. Search took **0.38** seconds.

**Shakespeare's Globe Theatre**, Bankside, Southwark, London
Shakespeare's Globe was founded by Sam Wanamaker and is dedicated to the experience and international understanding of Shakespeare in performance ...
Description: The official site includes images and archaeological evidence of the original Elizabethan circular...
Category: Arts > Architecture > ... > Building Types > Theaters and Cinemas
www.shakespeares-globe.org/ - 4k - Cached - Similar pages

**Shakespeare's Globe Theatre**, Bankside, Southwark, London
www.shakespeares-globe.org/navigation/frameset.htm - 1k - Cached - Similar pages
[ More results from www.shakespeares-globe.org ]

**Shakespeare's Globe Theatre**
About this site - Site guide, FAQ, site history and links. Shakespeare's Globe - A guide to the original Globe. The New Globe - The ...
Description: Provides background information on Shakespearean performance in original conditions. Includes guides...
Category: Kids and Teens > School Time > ... > Classics > Shakespeare, William
www.rdg.ac.uk/globe/ - 5k - Cached - Similar pages

Index of The Original Globe
Index for the Original Globe. Button link A general introduction Button link The archaeology of the Globe Button link The dimensions ...
www.rdg.ac.uk/globe/oldglobe/oldglobe_index.htm - 6k - Cached - Similar pages
[ More results from www.rdg.ac.uk ]

Shakespeare's Theatre
... If you are doing research on **Shakespeare's Globe Theatre** or are simply curious about the rebuilt Globe you cannot do better than to visit Shakespeare and the ...
shakespeare.palomar.edu/theatre.htm - 27k - Cached - Similar pages

Shakespeare Resource Center - Shakespeare's Globe
**Shakespeare's Globe Theatre** is a storied place. The original Globe ... its heyday. **Shakespeare's Globe Theatre** is a storied place. The ...
www.bardweb.net/globe.html - 12k - Cached - Similar pages

Sponsored Links
globe theatre
The Official Site For London. Find Info On All London Has To Offer.
www.visitlondon.com
See your message here...

Document: Done (1.04 secs)

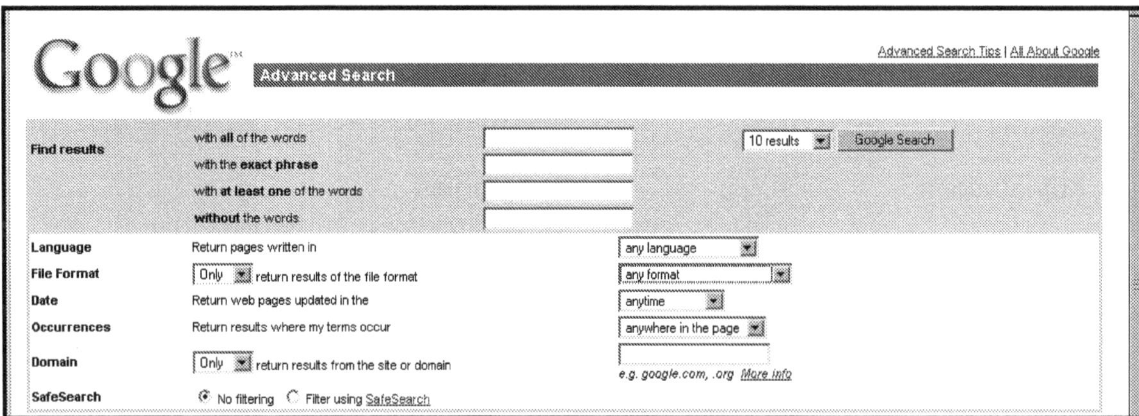
Google™ Advanced Search
Advanced Search Tips | All About Google

| | | | |
|---|---|---|---|
| **Find results** | with **all** of the words | | 10 results Google Search |
| | with the **exact phrase** | | |
| | with **at least one** of the words | | |
| | **without** the words | | |
| **Language** | Return pages written in | any language | |
| **File Format** | Only return results of the file format | any format | |
| **Date** | Return web pages updated in the | anytime | |
| **Occurrences** | Return results where my terms occur | anywhere in the page | |
| **Domain** | Only return results from the site or domain | e.g. google.com, .org More info | |
| **SafeSearch** | No filtering / Filter using SafeSearch | | |

# AltaVista Search (www.altavista.com)

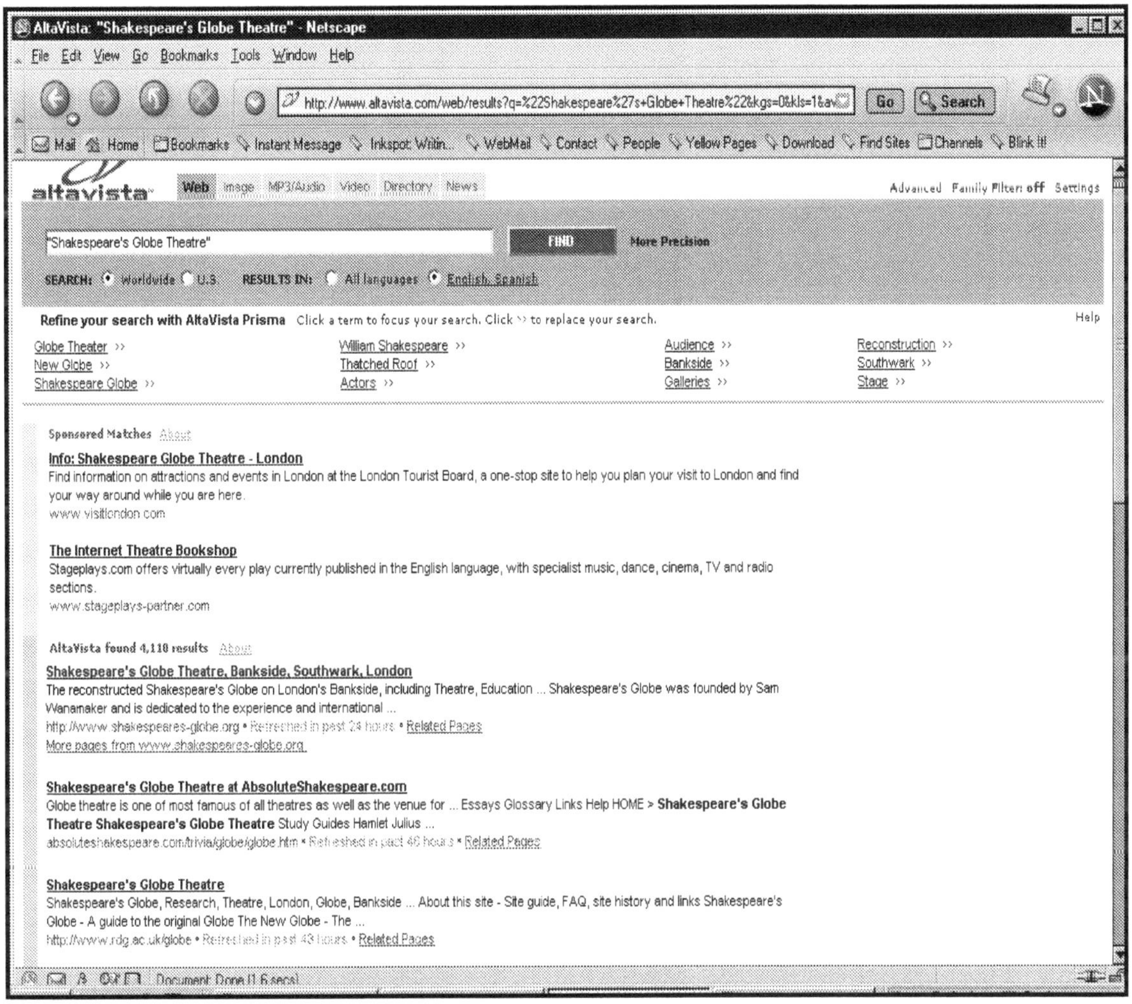

AltaVista: "Shakespeare's Globe Theatre" - Netscape

File Edit View Go Bookmarks Tools Window Help

http://www.altavista.com/web/results?q=%22Shakespeare%27s+Globe+Theatre%22&kgs=0&kls=1&av

Go Search

Mail Home Bookmarks Instant Message Inkspot: Writin... WebMail Contact People Yellow Pages Download Find Sites Channels Blink It!

altavista Web Image MP3/Audio Video Directory News Advanced Family Filter: off Settings

"Shakespeare's Globe Theatre" FIND More Precision

SEARCH: Worldwide U.S. RESULTS IN: All languages English, Spanish

**Refine your search with AltaVista Prisma** Click a term to focus your search. Click ›› to replace your search. Help

Globe Theater ›› William Shakespeare ›› Audience ›› Reconstruction ››
New Globe ›› Thatched Roof ›› Bankside ›› Southwark ››
Shakespeare Globe ›› Actors ›› Galleries ›› Stage ››

Sponsored Matches About

**Info: Shakespeare Globe Theatre - London**
Find information on attractions and events in London at the London Tourist Board, a one-stop site to help you plan your visit to London and find your way around while you are here.
www.visitlondon.com

**The Internet Theatre Bookshop**
Stageplays.com offers virtually every play currently published in the English language, with specialist music, dance, cinema, TV and radio sections.
www.stageplays-partner.com

AltaVista found 4,110 results About

**Shakespeare's Globe Theatre, Bankside, Southwark, London**
The reconstructed Shakespeare's Globe on London's Bankside, including Theatre, Education ... Shakespeare's Globe was founded by Sam Wanamaker and is dedicated to the experience and international ...
http://www.shakespeares-globe.org • Refreshed in past 24 hours • Related Pages
More pages from www.shakespeares-globe.org

**Shakespeare's Globe Theatre at AbsoluteShakespeare.com**
Globe theatre is one of most famous of all theatres as well as the venue for ... Essays Glossary Links Help HOME > **Shakespeare's Globe Theatre Shakespeare's Globe Theatre** Study Guides Hamlet Julius ...
absoluteshakespeare.com/trivia/globe/globe.htm • Refreshed in past 48 hours • Related Pages

**Shakespeare's Globe Theatre**
Shakespeare's Globe, Research, Theatre, London, Globe, Bankside ... About this site - Site guide, FAQ, site history and links Shakespeare's Globe - A guide to the original Globe The New Globe - The ...
http://www.rdg.ac.uk/globe • Refreshed in past 48 hours • Related Pages

Document: Done (1.6 secs)

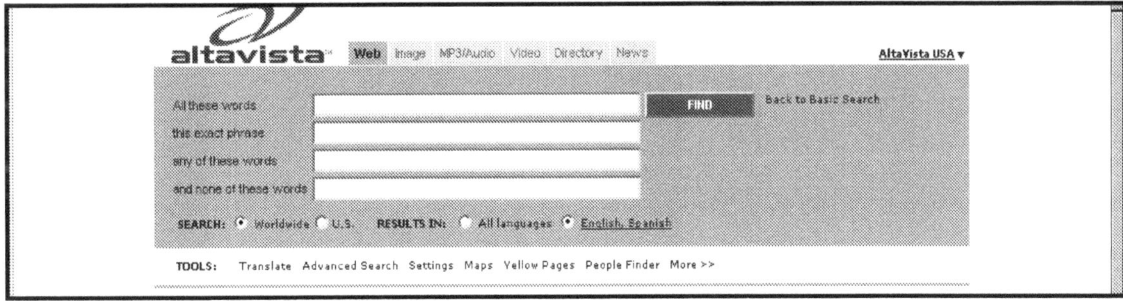

# Search Engine Comparison

| *Criteria* | *Yahooligans* | *Ask Jeeves for Kids* |
|---|---|---|
| Addresses Included | | |
| | | |
| Relevancy Rank or Score | | |
| | | |
| Site Summary (comment on whether it is useful or not) | | |
| | | |
| Option to search for related words or similar sites | | |
| | | |
| Size of homepage included | | |
| | | |
| Date of last update included | | |
| | | |
| Comments about usefulness of search engine | | |

# Search Engine Comparison

| *Criteria* | *Google* | *AltaVista* |
|---|---|---|
| Addresses Included | | |
| | | |
| Relevancy Rank or Score | | |
| | | |
| Site Summary (comment on whether it is useful or not) | | |
| | | |
| Option to search for related words or similar sites | | |
| | | |
| Size of homepage included | | |
| | | |
| Date of last update included | | |
| | | |
| Comments about usefulness of search engine | | |

# Search Engine Comparison

| *Criteria* | *MetaCrawler* | *Dogpile* |
|---|---|---|
| Addresses Included | | |
| | | |
| Relevancy Rank or Score | | |
| | | |
| Site Summary (comment on whether it is useful or not) | | |
| | | |
| Option to search for related words or similar sites | | |
| | | |
| Size of homepage included | | |
| | | |
| Date of last update included | | |
| | | |
| Comments about usefulness of search engine | | |

# What Search Terms To Use? 

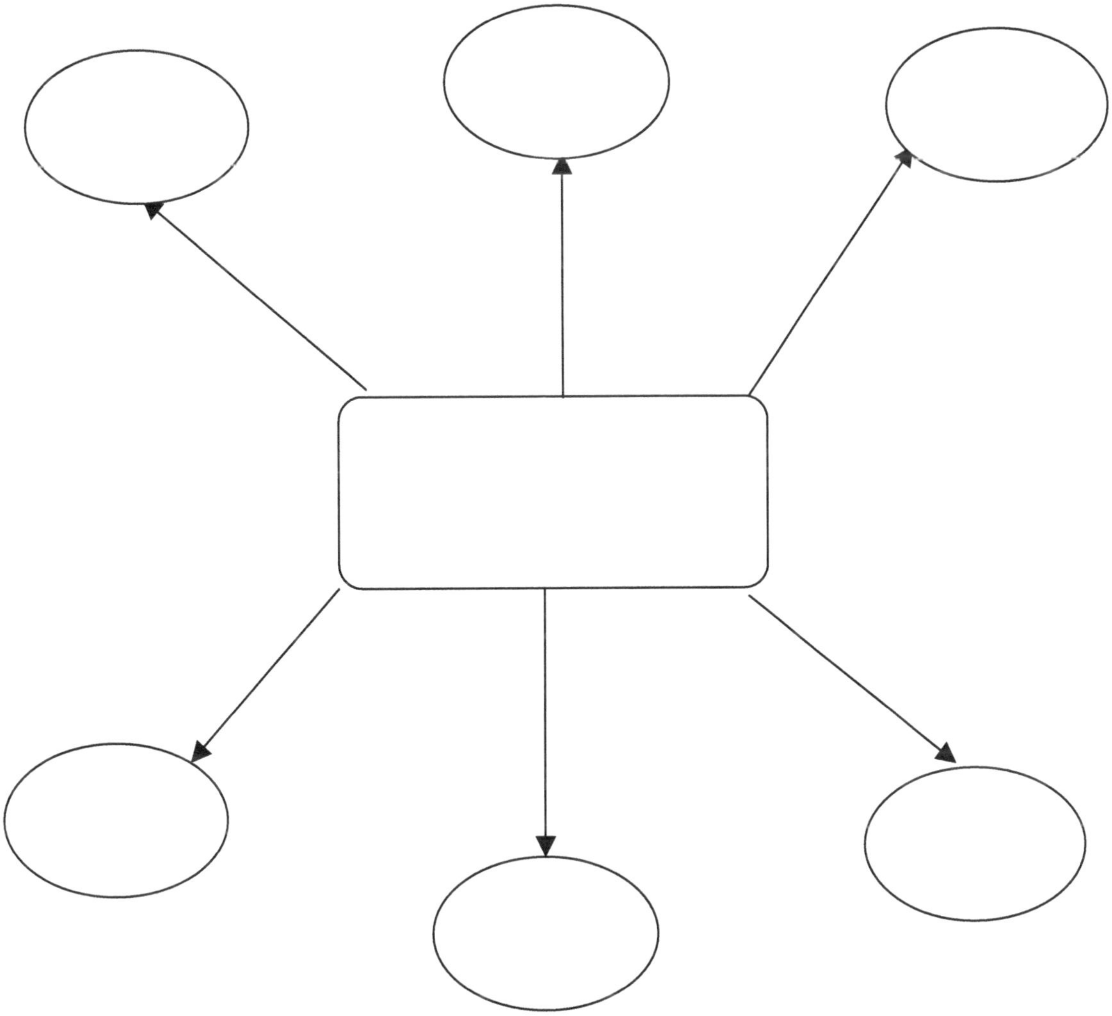

- Do I need to use phrases in my search?
- Do I need to use a " + " or a " – " in my search?
- Which search engine do I want to use first?
- How do I get to that search engine?

Joanne J. Troutner

# Content Evaluation Questions

- Who is the author?
- What credentials does this person have?
- Why should his/her information be considered reliable?
- What are the sources of the information?
- Is there a bibliography?
- Is the material at a suitable reading level for the audience?
- Has the information been updated recently?
- Is there a common link to the page from a recognized authority?
- Does the page provide other sources, which could be used to validate the information?
- Does the information appear biased?
- Does the author present multiple viewpoints of a controversial issue?
- Why was the information put on the Internet? For education, scholarly publication, or entertainment purposes?
- Would you have gotten the same information from an encyclopedia or other reference book?
- Does the page lead you to other useful Internet sites?
- Are you positive the information is true?
- What can you do to prove the information is true?
- Does the site where the information is housed, the domain, influence your opinion about the validity of the information?
- What evidence does the author give to support any claims or conclusions?
- Are charts and graphs included to support the claims or conclusions?

- If this is business/marketing web site, is it clear what company is sponsoring the site?
- Is there a way to verify the legitimate status of the company?
- If this is a news web site, is it clear what company is sponsoring the site?
- If this is a news web site, is it clear who wrote the article?
- If this is a news web site, is it clear who owns the copyright to the information?
- If this is an advocacy web site, is it clear what organization is sponsoring the site?
- Is there a link to the goals of the organization sponsoring the advocacy web site?
- Is there a statement that the web site has the official approval of the advocacy organization?
- Is it clear that the national or local chapter of the organization sponsors the advocacy site?

*Either have students brainstorm additions to this list or have students brainstorm their own list of evaluation criteria.*

*Discuss what elements need to be added to Internet information evaluations that are not included when evaluating traditional reference sources.*

Visit these web sites for more information on web site evaluation—

- Teaching Critical Evaluation Skills for WWW Resources
- //www2.widener.edu/Wolfgram-Memorial-Library/webevaluation/webeval.htmThinking Critically about WWW Resources //www.library.ucla.edu/libraries/college/help/critical/index.htm

# Content Evaluation-Elementary

Look at the attached page or view the one on the screen and answer the questions.

| | | |
|---|---|---|
| ✓ Can you tell who is the author? | Yes | No |
| ✓ Are you sure the information is true? | Yes | No |
| ✓ Can you find another source to prove the information is true? | Yes | No |
| ✓ Has the information been changed recently? | Yes | No |
| ✓ Could you have gotten the same information from an encyclopedia? | Yes | No |
| ✓ Is the information presented from just one point of view? | Yes | No |
| ✓ Does the author have qualifications to prove his/her work is trustworthy? | Yes | No |
| ✓ Is there a list of resources? | Yes | No |
| ✓ Does the site where the information is housed, the domain, influence your opinion about the validity of the information? | Yes | No |
| ✓ Does the information appear biased? | Yes | No |
| ✓ Can you read the material easily? | Yes | No |
| ✓ Are charts or graphs included to support the information? | Yes | No |

✎ Write a paragraph to explain why another student should or should not use this Internet site as a source of information for his/her project.

# Content Evaluation-Secondary

Look at the attached page or view the one on the screen and answer the questions.

| | | |
|---|---|---|
| ✓ Can you tell who is the author? | Yes | No |
| ✓ Are you sure the information is true? | Yes | No |
| ✓ Can you find another source to prove the information is true? | Yes | No |
| ✓ Has the information been changed recently? | Yes | No |
| ✓ Could you have gotten the same information from an encyclopedia? | Yes | No |
| ✓ Is the information presented from just one point of view? | Yes | No |
| ✓ Does the author have credentials to prove his/her work is reliable? | Yes | No |
| ✓ Is there a common link to the page from a recognized authority? | Yes | No |
| ✓ Is there a bibliography? | Yes | No |
| ✓ Does the site where the information is housed, the domain, influence your opinion about the validity of the information? | Yes | No |
| ✓ Does the information appear biased? | Yes | No |
| ✓ Is the material at a suitable reading level for the audience? | Yes | No |
| ✓ Are charts or graphs included to support the claims or conclusions? | Yes | No |

✎ Write a paragraph to explain why another student should or should not use this Internet site as a source of information for his/her project.

Joanne J. Troutner

# Web Design Criteria

- Does the page take a long time to load?
- Does the page fit on one screen?
- If the page is not one screen long, are there buttons to get other parts of the it?
- Are the graphics or pictures useful or just decoration?
- Are the icons useful?
- Is the spelling correct?
- Can you navigate to other links easily?
- Are the other links logical?
- Are the other links useful?
- Are the links clearly marked and explained?
- Can you get back to the index or menu page easily from a linked page?
- Is the author's name included?
- Is the author's e-mail address included?
- Is a date available to tell the last time the information was changed?
- Is the format readable with the web browser you are using?
- If you don't load the graphics are text descriptions included?
- Is the format of the pages consistent?

Look at this web site for more information—

Web Design //www.esc20.net/techserv/workshops/webdesign/

# Web Design Evaluation–Elementary

Look at the attached web pages or view the ones on the screen and answer the questions for each homepage.

| | | |
|---|---|---|
| ♦ Are the pictures helpful? | Yes | No |
| ♦ Is the spelling correct? | Yes | No |
| ♦ Are the links easy to find? | Yes | No |
| ♦ Is the author's name included? | Yes | No |
| ♦ Does the page take a long time to load? | Yes | No |
| ♦ Is there an option to have frames or no frames? | Yes | No |
| ♦ Do the links make sense and follow in order? | Yes | No |
| ♦ Are the links useful? | Yes | No |
| ♦ Is the author's e-mail address included? | Yes | No |
| ♦ Is the format readable with the web browser you are using? | Yes | No |
| ♦ Can you get back to the index or menu page easily from a linked page? | Yes | No |
| ♦ Are the icons useful? | Yes | No |

✐ Write a paragraph to tell what you would change or add to make this page better.

Joanne J. Troutner

# Web Design Evaluation–Secondary

Look at the attached web pages or view the ones on the screen and answer the questions for each homepage.

| | | |
|---|---|---|
| ♦ Are the pictures helpful? | Yes | No |
| ♦ Is the spelling correct? | Yes | No |
| ♦ Are the links easy to find? | Yes | No |
| ♦ Is the author's name included? | Yes | No |
| ♦ Does the page take a long time to load? | Yes | No |
| ♦ Is there an option to have frames or no frames? | Yes | No |
| ♦ Are the links logical? | Yes | No |
| ♦ Are the links useful? | Yes | No |
| ♦ Is the author's e-mail address included? | Yes | No |
| ♦ Is the format readable with the web browser you are using? | Yes | No |
| ♦ Can you get back to the index or menu page easily from a linked page? | Yes | No |
| ♦ Are the icons useful? | Yes | No |

✐ Write a paragraph to tell what you would change or add to make this page better.

# News Source Comparison

| *Criteria* | *NY Times* | *USA Today* |
|---|---|---|
| Information Current | | |
| | | |
| Author Cited/Credible | | |
| | | |
| Visual Design | | |
| | | |
| Links to Related Sources Relevant/Useful | | |
| | | |
| Readability | | |
| | | |
| Pictures Useful | | |
| | | |
| Comments about other features/factors | | |

# Bogus Web Sites--Information Literacy Tools

- ✓ Burmese Mountain Dog—
  http://lme.mnsu.edu/akcj3/bmd.html
  Look at the picture and pay close attention to the characteristics of the breed

- ✓ Mankato, MN Homepage—
  http://www.lme.mnsu.edu/mankato/mankato.html
  Look closely and the pictures

- ✓ Feline Reactions to Bearded Men—
  http://www.improb.com/airchives/classical/cat/cat.html
  Examine the premise of the study

- ✓ British Parliament Accused of Plagiarizing—
  http://www.theonion.com/onion3628/parliament_plagiarizes.html
  Examine the news story closely

- ✓ California's Velcro Crop Under Challenge—
  http://www.umbachconsulting.com/miscellany/velcro.html
  Look at the charts and scholarly writing

- ✓ Study of Holocaust Revisionism—
  http://pubweb.acns.nwu.edu/~abutz/di/intro.html
  A very different look at the Holocaust

- ✓ DHMO
  http://www.dhmo.org
  Look at the dangers of good old $H_20$ or water

# Using Primary Source Material

**Questions to Ask—**

- ✓ Who created the source and why?
- ✓ Did the recorder have firsthand knowledge of the event?
- ✓ Was the recorder a neutral party?
- ✓ Was the source meant to be public or private?
- ✓ For whom was the source created?
- ✓ Under what circumstances was the source created?
- ✓ Why was the image created?
- ✓ What is the point of view of the image?
- ✓ How long after the event was the image or the account created?

**Teaching Using Primary Source Materials—**

| | |
|---|---|
| Interpreting Primary Sources | //www.si.umich.edu/SPIES/lounge-sources.html |
| | |
| Using Primary Sources in the Classroom | //memory.loc.gov/ammem/ndlpedu/lessons/primary.html |

**Primary Source Material Sites—**

| | |
|---|---|
| Spy Letters of the American Revolution | //www.si.umich.edu/SPIES/ |
| | |
| Images of American Political History | //teachpol.tcnj.edu/amer_pol_hist/ |
| | |
| Ad*Access | //scriptorium.lib.duke.edu/adaccess/browse.html |
| | |
| Archiving Early America | //earlyamerica.com |
| | |
| George Rarey's Journals of the 379th Fighter Squadron (WWII) | //www.rareybird.com/ |
| | |
| Letters from an Iowa Soldier in the Civil War | //www.civilwarletters.com/home.html |
| | |
| National Archives Digital Classroom | //www.archives.gov/digital_classroom/ |
| | |
| National Archives of Canada | //www.archives.ca/ |

# Primary Source Material Evaluation

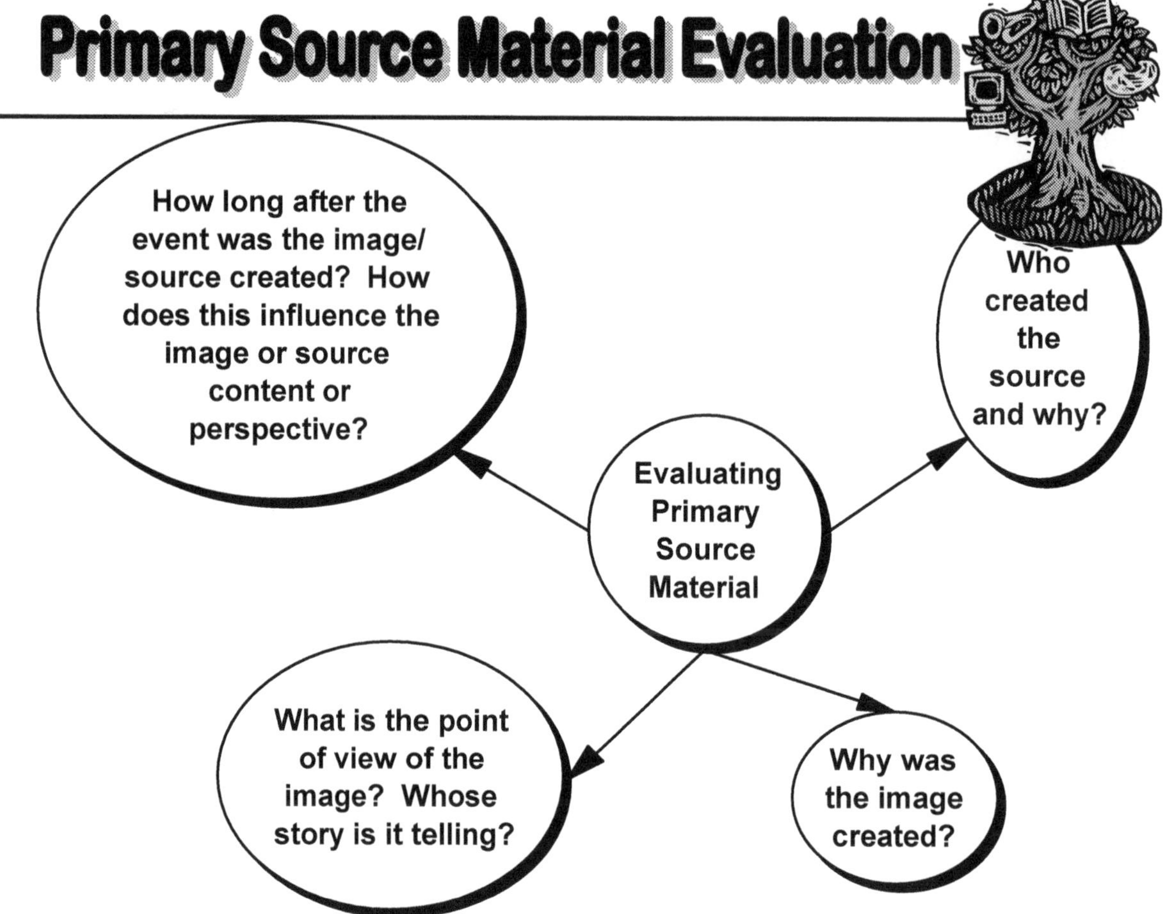


Answer the questions below—

# Document Analysis

What is the document—newspaper, letter, patent, memorandum, map, telegram, press release, report, ad, Congressional record, census report?

Are there any unique physical qualities—interesting letterhead, handwritten, typed, seals, notations, "RECEIVED" stamp?

What is the date of the document?
Who is the author/creator of the document? What is his/her position or title?
Who was the intended audience for the document?
List three things the author said that you think are important.

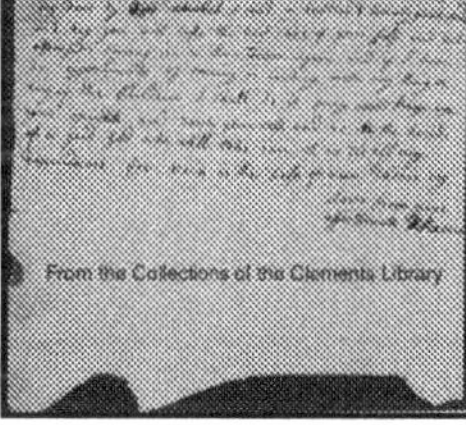


http://www.si.umich.edu/SPIES/index-gallery.html

1.

2.

3.

Why do you think this document was written?
What evidence in the document illustrates why it was written? Quote from the document.

List two things the document tells you about life at the time it was written.

1.

2.

What a question to the author that is still unanswered by the document.

Joanne J. Troutner

# Photo Analysis

Observation—

Study the photograph as a whole. Form an overall impression of the picture. Next, divide the photo into quarters. Study each section to see what new details you find.

Use the chart to list items in the photograph.

| People | Objects | Activities |
|---|---|---|
| | | |
| | | |
| | | |
| | | |
| | | |
| | | |
| | | |

Based on what you observed, list three things you might infer from the photograph.

1.

2.

3.

What questions does this photograph raise in your mind?

Child Laborers in Indiana Glass Works, Midnight, Indiana. 1908. Photographer, Lewis W. Hine

Public Domain Image from National Archives and Records Administration

http://teachpol.tcnj.edu/amer_pol_hist/thumbnail272.html

# Plagiarism Prevention Tips

⇒ Consider having students take notes in two colors of ink. Black ink for information they are simply recording. Green ink for information that is their own or constructed.

⇒ Have students turn in electronic references with paper or project.

⇒ Use a search engine such as Alta Vista, Google and type in the unique phrase from the student's paper.

⇒ Use the materials found at the following web sites for classroom activities.

| | |
|---|---|
| Sample Plagiarized Papers | //www.plagiarized.com/workshop.shtml |
| | |
| CyberCheats | //reference.camden.lib.nj.us/classes/garwood/cybercheats |
| | |
| Internet Paper Mill Site Bibliography | //www.coastal.edu/library/mills2.htm |
| | |
| Handouts on Paraphrasing and Using Quotations | //www.library.ualberta.ca/guides/plagiarism/handouts.html |
| | |
| Student Self Test | //ec.hku.hk/plagiarism/self_test.htm |
| | |
| Avoiding Plagiarism | //owl.english.purdue.edu/handouts/research/r_plagiar.html |

⇒ Visit TurnItIn.Com, //www.turnitin.com/, and use the free one month trial, which will provide up to 5 separate reports.

+++-

# Projects & Assessment Ideas

Use this section to:

- ✓ Gather ideas for assessing technology oriented projects
- ✓ Gain already developed curriculum based projects
- ✓ Use the ideas presented as springboards for your own projects

# Project Development

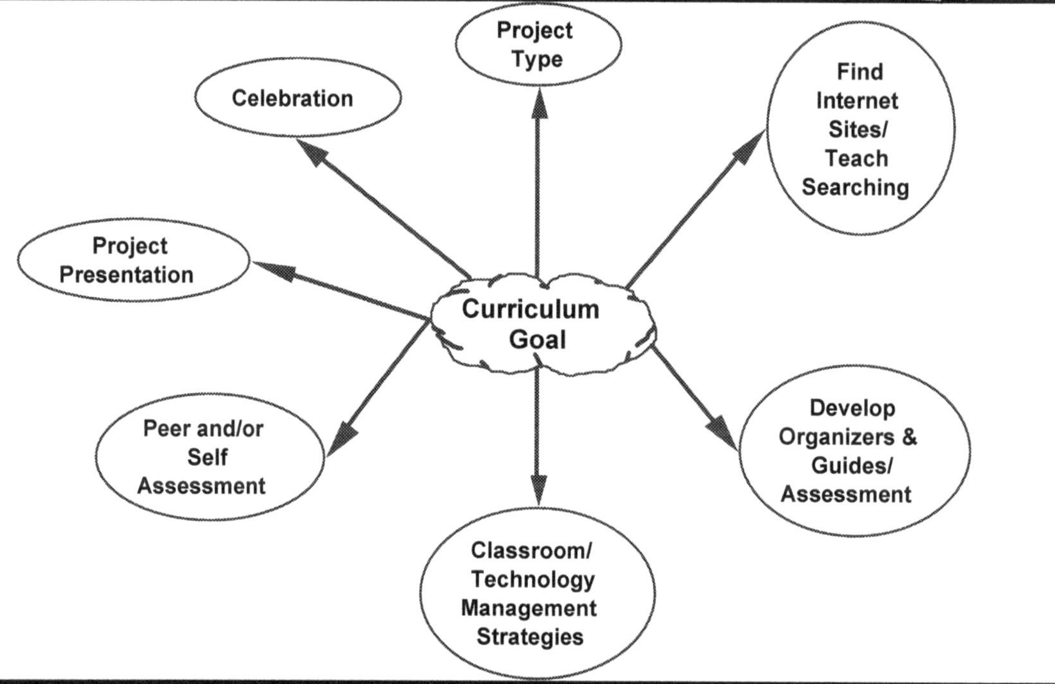


1. Decide on curriculum goal.
2. What project type(s) will the students develop?
3. Will you provide a list of Internet sites for the students?
4. How will you teach searching skills?
5. Develop the advanced organizers/guides and assessment strategies.
6. Think through the classroom/technology management strategies you will need to use
7. Provide time for peer and/or self assessment.
8. Do project presentations.
9. Celebrate the success!!!!!

# Project Definitions

⇒ *Virtual Tours*

This option has a list of bookmarks or a single site that either the teacher or students select. Questions, activities, and points of interest are suggested for the user. A graphic organizer or some sort of itinerary is developed to guide the user through the visit and for recording information

⇒ *Hotlist/Bookmark List*

This is a list of bookmarks on a specific topic. It can be done in print format, designed as a web page, or a set of bookmarks exported to a disk. This format helps acquaint the students with the material available on a specific topic. You may also choose to have the students use their searching skills and develop their own hotlists.

⇒ *Scavenger Hunt/Treasure Hunt*

This option has either the teacher or the students develop content knowledge about the subject by searching exemplary Internet sites for answers to a series of questions. The questions need to help the user gather knowledge about the topic and guide him toward a deeper vein of thought. Do not make this a hunt for unrelated snippets of knowledge about a topic. Include a final question, which has the user synthesize the information gathered.

⇒ *E-Mail Projects*

This Internet experience is the electronic version of having pen pals. Referred to as key pals, students exchange letters with students in different areas of the United States or the world via Internet e-mail.

⇒ *Collaborative Projects*

This option takes the e-mail project a step further. Here students work with data collection and analysis, develop a joint student publication, or participate in a virtual adventure such as MayaQuest.

⇒ *WebQuests*

This option is "an inquiry-oriented activity in which some or all of the information that learners interact with comes from resources on the Internet." (Bernie Dodge, http://edweb.sdsu.edu/courses/edtec596/about_webquests.html)

The WebQuest presents a challenging task, scenario, or problem for the students to solve. The resources needed to complete the task are included in the WebQuest along with a description of the process to be used and some learning guidance. The conclusion asks the user to synthesize the information gathered and to complete the task. WebQuests can range from 1 - 3 class periods up to a month or yearlong project.

⇒ *Interdisciplinary Projects*

This option allows the students to pick from a number of activities arranged around a theme, which touches various disciplines. A group presentation option is included in each project.

+---

# Questions to Ask About Internet Projects

- What educational purpose do you have in mind?
- Why is the Internet a good resource for accomplishing this purpose?
- What preparation have you done to find appropriate sites?
- Are you providing your students with a set of bookmarks or addresses to use for their searches?
- What search strategies will you or your students use?
- How are you going to handle either one point of access with your class or multiple points of access?
- What preparation have you given the students for evaluating the information they find?
- How will you maximize instructional time?
- How will you insure compliance with the school's Internet policy?
- What will you do to insure that your students have a safe Internet experience?
- How will you assess the project?

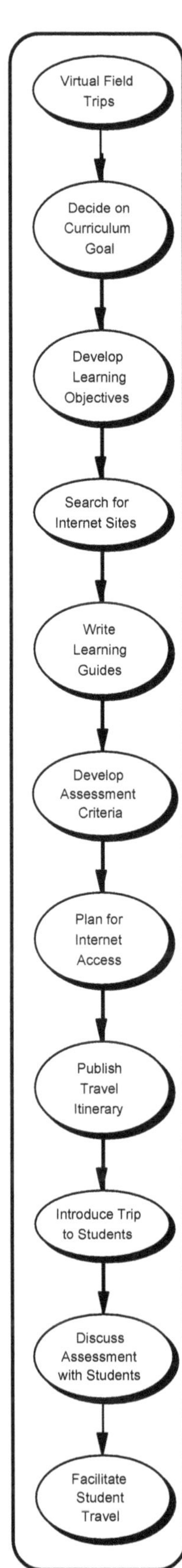


# Developing a Virtual Field Trip

Why use virtual field trips?

- ✓ Preparation for a real field trip
- ✓ Take students to a place they may never visit
- ✓ Provide the same learning experience for the entire class
- ✓ Develop interest in a topic

Assessment Ideas—

- ✓ Provide a set of questions to be answered
- ✓ Have students write a paragraph or two to describe what they learned
- ✓ How will you know students have reached the learning objectives when you see it?

Classroom Management Tips—

- ✓ Have students work in pairs
- ✓ Provide bookmark or simple web page with sites to use
- ✓ Provide clear expectations
- ✓ Provide learning guides for students

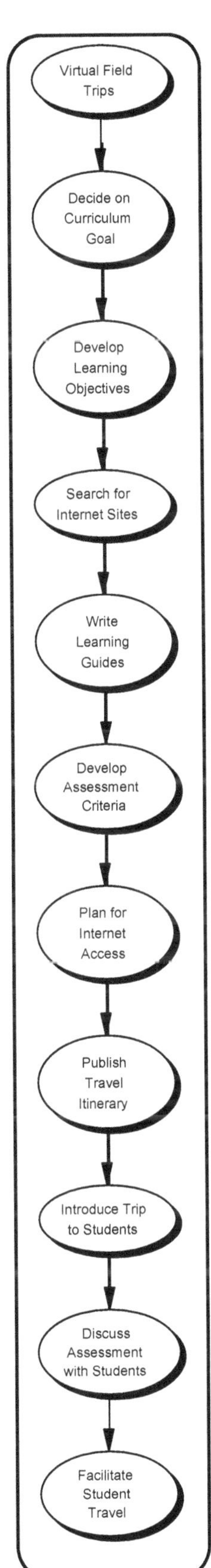


# Virtual Field Trip to Field Museum

Curriculum Goal—
Understand the connection between natural science and historical events

Learning Objectives—
- ✓ Gather information from a web site
- ✓ Provide advanced organizer for exhibits
- ✓ Become prepared for finding exhibits

Search for Internet Sites—
- ✓ Use Metacrawler and search for phrase "Field Museum"
- ✓ Make bookmarks (will need to distribute on network) //www.fmnh.org

Write Learning Guides—
- ✓ Contact Info
- ✓ Print Floor Plans
- ✓ Questions for Two Exhibits
- ✓ Map Activity Answer Spaces

Assessment Criteria—
- ✓ Worked well with partner
- ✓ Contact information home to parents
- ✓ Able to discuss assigned exhibit in class

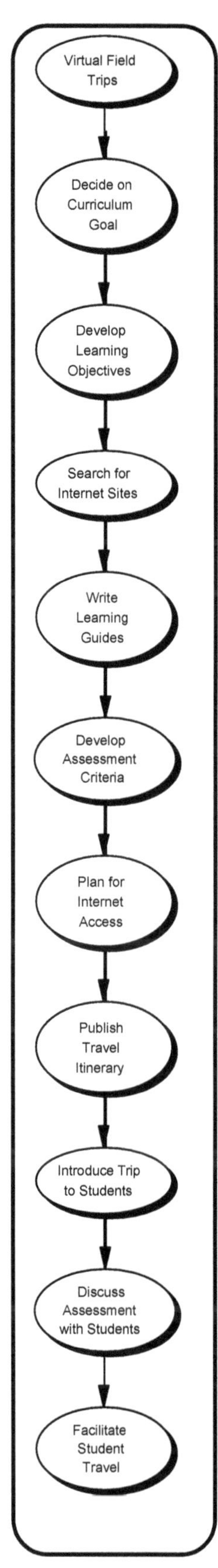


Plan for Internet Access—

- ✓ Seek copyright permission to download site
- ✓ Place downloaded site information on network and CD ROM
- ✓ Schedule computer lab for one class period

Publish Travel Itinerary—

- ✓ Put activity sheet on network for student access
- ✓ Explain time expectations

Introduce to Students—

- ✓ Explain expectations
- ✓ Set up partners
- ✓ Reinforce time line

Discuss Assessment with Students—

- ✓ Go over scoring rubric for team/partner work
- ✓ Talk about parent contact to see if emergency info makes it home
- ✓ Go over scoring rubric for classroom discussion

# Virtual Field Trip to Field Museum

Name:________________________________________________

Date:____________________________ Period:__________________

Directions—Develop driving directions using your atlas. Write at the bottom of the 2nd page.

| Bottom Floor | Print floor plan—put X by Bottom Floor when done |
|---|---|
| | |
| Lunch Location | |
| | |
| Contact Information | |
| | |
| First Floor | Print floor plan—put X by First Floor when done |
| | |
| 1st Exhibit | |
| | |
| Question 1 | |
| | |

| Question 2 | |
|---|---|
| | |
| 2nd Exhibit | |
| | |
| Question 1 | |
| | |
| Question 2 | |

---

Directions—

# Virtual Field Trips

⇒ Audience: Elementary school students

⇒ Uses: Provide students with the option to visit places they may never see

Use as a pre-visit activity for field trip

⇒ Curriculum Areas: Geography
Language Arts

| • Field Museum of Natural History, Chicago, Illinois | //www.fmnh.org |
|---|---|

*Have students gather the following information from the Field Museum web site in preparation for a real field trip.*

- Where is the museum currently located?
- When was the collection started?
- Which exhibit will you find information about mummies? Where is it located in the museum?
- Which part of the museum will you visit to find information that compares Eskimos and Northwest Coast Indians?
- Can you find information on the art lacquer of Japan? If so, where in the museum can you find this exhibit?
- What country houses the people who live at the highest inhabited altitude on earth?
- Use a map of Chicago to plan your travel once you arrive in the city. See if the museum web site can help you.
- Where can you eat lunch during your trip?

Joanne J. Troutner

# Virtual Aquarium Tours

**Objectives:**

| | |
|---|---|
| ⇒ Technology | to use search engines to gather sites for a complex project |
| | to access specific sites and use them as the starting place for gathering information |
| | |
| ⇒ Core Curriculum | to practice presentation developing skills |
| | to practice communications skills—oral and written |
| | to develop visual presentations |
| | to learn about the various ocean life included in a aquarium |
| | to learn about a specific aquarium and environment |
| | to practice math computation |
| | to develop a process leading to a final event |
| | |
| ⇒ Research/Reference | to gather information needed for a complex project |
| | to disseminate information in various forms |

**Internet Sources:**

Various Internet search engines should reveal some of the following sites

| | |
|---|---|
| ⇒ Monterey Bay E-quarium | http://www.mbayaq.org/ |
| ⇒ Waikiki Aquarium | http://www.mic.hawaii.edu/aquarium/ |
| ⇒ Oregon Coast Aquarium | http://www.aquarium.org:80/ |
| ⇒ Florida Aquarium | http://www.flaquarium.net/ |
| ⇒ Tennessee Aquarium | http://www.tennis.org/ |
| ⇒ National Aquarium in Baltimore | http://www.aqua.org/ |

**Other Resources:**

Library resources ocean life, aquariums, and the environment

**Activity:**

Have the students create a virtual tour of one aquarium. The students need to create the various activities, exhibits, and guides, which would enhance this virtual tour. These components may be ocean life trading cards, a list of questions to answer while touring, a set of hints of things to see, a brochure detailing the tour, a PowerPoint tour, or other items.

Include a peer assessment component half-way through the work time to help insure that students are progressing adequately.

Allow time for student sharing of the various exhibits.

**Assessment Ideas:**

Have teachers and/or students who are studying ocean life and the environment visit the exhibit and critique it.

Use the sample assessment rubric as a start for developing your own rubric.

Joanne J. Troutner

# *Virtual Aquarium Tour Project*

Your role as a virtual tour creator for an aquarium is to accomplish the following:

1. Use at least three search engines or one per group member to gather sites useful for developing your tour. You may choose to use on the aquarium sites provided by your teacher as a starting point.

2. Divide up the sites and information. Then begin deciding which pieces need to be included in your tour. Be sure to evaluate the information and make certain you feel it is creditable. Use the virtual tour planning sheet, trading card activity, and your knowledge about evaluating information to accomplish this task.

3. After you have decided on the activities and materials needed for your virtual tour, begin work on the presentation your group will develop. Use the presentation planning chart to help keep track of decisions.

4. Now, assemble the pieces of your tour into a complete draft.

5. Do a trial tour and complete a peer assessment. Also consider having either fellow students, a teacher, or another adult take your tour and provide you with feedback.

6. Refine/revise your tour.

7. See that handouts are copied, the necessary hardware is available, proper software is loaded, and have a backup copy of your exhibit.

# Virtual Tour Planning Sheet

List the major topics your group needs to cover in this tour.

1.

2.

3.

4.

5.

6.

Brainstorm a list of search terms your group needs to use.

# Virtual Tour Planning Chart

| Site | Address | Reason(s) to Include in the Tour |
|---|---|---|
| | | |
| | | |
| | | |
| | | |
| | | |
| | | |

## Hint Sheet Chart

| Exhibit Location | What Not to Miss/ Question to Answer/ Information to Find |
|---|---|
| | |
| | |
| | |
| | |

# Trading Card Activity

Draw a paper mock-up of your trading card before you develop it. Ask the following questions.

1. Is the layout appealing?

2. What font or typestyle will you use?

3. What size type will you use?

4. Will you use bold, italics, or underline to emphasize any information?

Be sure your trading card includes the following:

◊ The type of ocean life
◊ The name of the animal
◊ The life cycle of the animal
◊ A picture of the animal
◊ The food eaten by the animal
◊ Places where further information can be found

# Presentation Planning Chart

| Topic | Who |
|---|---|
| | |
| | |
| | |
| | |
| | |
| | |
| | |
| | |
| | |
| | |
| | |
| | |
| | |
| | |
| | |

Joanne J. Troutner

# A Virtual Trip To Mexico

| | |
|---|---|
| ⇒ Audience: | Middle and high school students |
| ⇒ Uses: | Provide an introduction to Mexico<br>Give students a brief look at modern day Mexico |
| ⇒ Curriculum Area: | Social Studies |
| ⇒ NCSS Strands: | (1) Culture and (3) People, Places, and Environments |

| | |
|---|---|
| • ***National Geographic Magazine*** | //www.nationalgeographic.com/features/96/mexico/index.html |

***First visit Mexico City.***

1. Listen to the Real Audio comments from the author. With what US city does he compare Mexico City?

2. What act is credited with causing the worst recession in Mexico in decades? Why would this event cause a recession?

3. Why do you think so many people live in Mexico City?

***Visit the Daily Dispatches for Mexico City.***

4. What insights do these give you about the culture and life in Mexico City? Describe the visit to the Merced food market.

***Next visit Tijuana.***

5. What are the major differences between the United States and Mexico along this border?

6. What causes the rush across the Mexican border to the United States? How would you solve this problem?

***Next visit the Heartland of Mexico.***

7. Describe the two things found here which illustrate the Mexican culture.

***Finally, visit Chiapas.***

8. What group of Maya Indians lives in this region?

9. Why are these people fighting the Mexican government?

10. Why would the leader use the Internet to post his manifestos?

---

## *Assessment Ideas*

- ✓ Have students report orally on the aspect of modern Mexico which most interested them.
- ✓ Provide current information on the Zapatistas movement and have students react either verbally or in writing.
- ✓ Gather information on population growth of Mexico City and discuss the impact on the city.
- ✓ Have students write a short diary entry about one of the places visited in the virtual trip.
- ✓ Have students rate their ability to stay on task while using the Internet.

Have students work in pairs to take this virtual tour. This will help students with the higher level questions included and provide practice in teamwork.

Joanne J. Troutner

# Visiting Shakespeare's England

***Objectives:***

| | |
|---|---|
| ⇒ Technology | to use search engines to gather a number of sites for a complex project<br>to access specific sites and use them as the starting place for gathering information |
| ⇒ Core Curriculum | to practice presentation developing skills<br>to practice communications skills—oral and written<br>to develop visual presentations<br>to learn about the literature of William Shakespeare<br>to gain information about life in England during the time of Shakespeare<br>to develop a process leading to a final event |
| ⇒ Research/Reference | to gather information needed for a complex project<br>to disseminate information in various forms |

***Internet Sources:***

Various Internet search engines, which should reveal some of the following sites

| | |
|---|---|
| ⇒ Mr. William Shakespeare and the Internet | //shakespeare.palomar.edu/ |
| ⇒ Shakespeare Birthplace Trust | //www.shakespeare.org.uk/ |
| ⇒ Shakespeare and the Globe Theatre | //www.rdg.ac.uk/globe/ |
| ⇒ Rivendell's Shakespeare Page | //www.watson.org/%7Eleigh/ shakespeare.html |
| ⇒ Shakespeare Alive | //ns2.d20.co.edu/kadets/shakespeare/ |
| ⇒ Virtual Renaissance | //www.twingroves.district96.k12. il.us/ Renaissance/VirtualRen.html |

***Other Resources:***

Library resources on Shakespeare and England at that time

**Activity:**

Have the students create a virtual tour for others designed to learn about Shakespeare, his life in Stratford-on-Avon, his life in London, the Globe Theatre. The tour should be a guided list of web addresses with hints for each site about items not to miss. Then, have the students research and design a real trip to England to study Shakespeare and the places visited on the virtual tour.

Include a peer assessment component half-way through the work time to help insure that students are progressing adequately.

Allow time for student sharing about the various virtual and real tours.

Joanne J. Troutner

# Visiting Shakespeare's England Project

Your role as a tour guide group is to accomplish the following:

1. Use at least three search engines or one per group member to gather sites for use in your virtual tour about Shakespeare. Remember that you need to include information about Shakespeare, his life in Stratford-on-Avon, his life in London, the Globe Theatre, and the people of that time.

2. Divide up the sites and begin searching for those you want to recommend for your virtual tour. Use the Virtual Tour chart to help you organize your information.

3. After you have decided on the sites for the virtual tour, begin work on the hint sheet for each site. Consider what things you want the viewers to gather or learn at each site. You will want to include at least two things the viewer needs to find or questions to be answered. You are welcome to do more. Focus on what the viewer will find interesting or what will help the viewer understand the life of Shakespeare better. Use the Hint Sheet chart to help you organize your information for this task.

4. Now, begin to gather information from the Internet and other references for planning the real trip. Use the planning sheet and budget sheet to organize your information and presentation designed to encourage people to take your tour.

**Assessment Ideas:**

⇒ Have teachers and/or students who are studying Shakespeare take the virtual tour and critique it.

⇒ Have a travel agent watch the presentations on the real trips and comment.

⇒ Use the sample assessment rubric as a start for developing your own rubric.

## Virtual Tour Planning Sheet

List the major topics your group needs to cover in the tour.

1.

2.

3.

4.

5.

6.

Brainstorm a list of search terms your group needs to use.

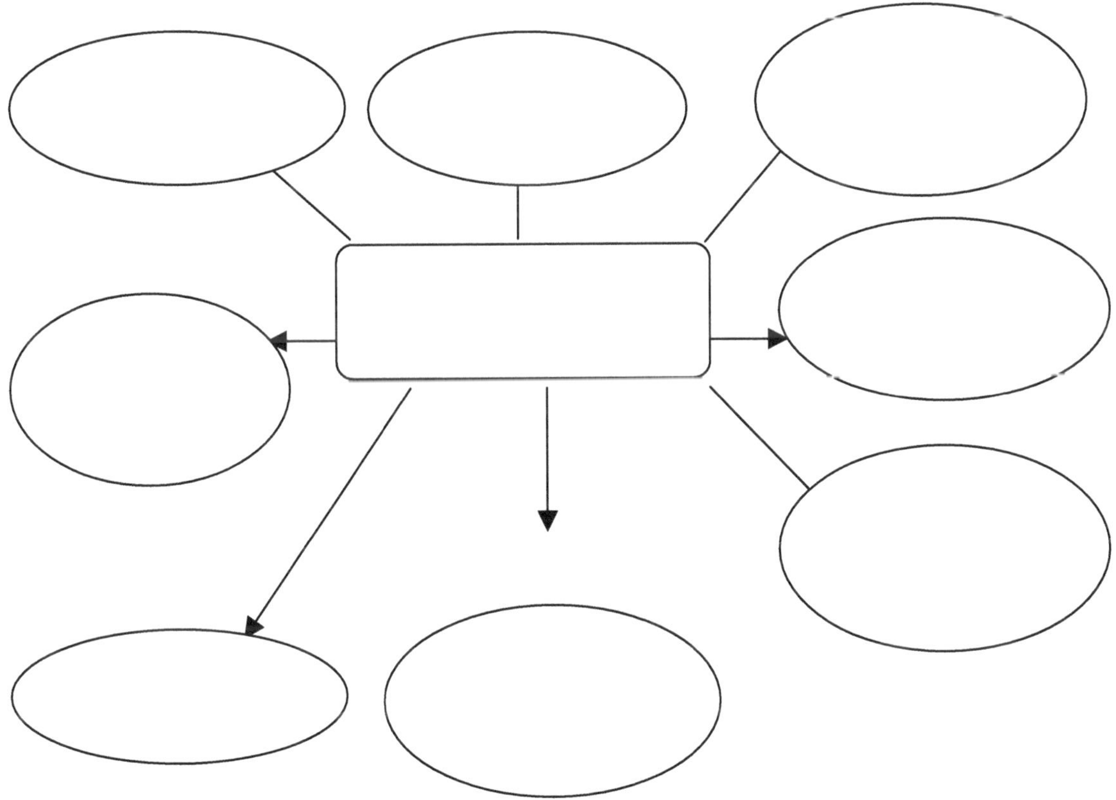

# Virtual Tour Chart

| Site | Address | Reason(s) to Include on Tour |
|---|---|---|
| | | |
| | | |
| | | |
| | | |
| | | |

# Hint Sheet Chart

| Site | Address | What Not to Miss/ Question to Answer/ Information to Find |
|---|---|---|
| | | |
| | | |
| | | |
| | | |
| | | |

# Visiting Shakespeare's England for Real

1. Now you are ready to plan a real trip to England and visit the places your found for the virtual tour.

2. Begin by getting airfare information at http://www.travelocity.com. Find the best price you can.

3. Now look for a place to stay in each place you visit. Try searching with the name of the town and lodging.

4. Next look at the Virtual Tourist site, http://www.virtualtourist.com/vt//, to find more information and places to suggest for meals.

5. What landmarks should your tour group see? Find information on these sites, directions, and costs.

6. Put together a travel package for your group including all the pricing information, a persuasive presentation to entice people to select your tour, and an information sheet with travel tips on passports, money, etc. How you choose to present this is up to your group. You may want to use the Presentation Planning chart to help organize your efforts.

7. You will present your tour package to the entire class as a culminating activity.

8. Do a trial run of your presentation and complete a peer assessment.

9. Refine/revise your presentation.

10. Practice your presentation.

11. See that handouts are copied, the necessary hardware is available, proper software is loaded, and have a backup copy of your presentation.

# Presentation Planning Chart

| Topic | Who |
| --- | --- |
| | |
| | |
| | |
| | |
| | |
| | |
| | |
| | |
| | |
| | |
| | |
| | |
| | |
| | |
| | |
| | |
| | |
| | |

Joanne J. Troutner

# Traveling Lewis & Clark's Trail

***Objectives:***

| | |
|---|---|
| ⇒ Technology | to use search engines to gather a number of sites for a complex project<br>to access specific sites and use them as the starting place for gathering information |
| ⇒ Core Curriculum | to practice presentation developing skills<br>to practice communications skills—oral and written<br>to develop visual presentations<br>to learn about the travels of Lewis and Clark<br>to gain information about life in the United States during the time of Lewis and Clark<br>to develop a process leading to a final event |
| ⇒ Research/Reference | to gather information needed for a complex project<br>to disseminate information in various forms |
| ⇒ NCSS Strands | (2) Time, Continuity, and Change |

***Resources:***

| | |
|---|---|
| ⇒ Welcome to the Lewis & Clark National Historic Trail | //www.nps.gov/lecl/welcome.htm |
| ⇒ PBS Online—Lewis & Clark | //www.pbs.org/lewisandclark/ |
| ⇒ Lewis and Clark—Lost Missouri | //magma.nationalgeographic.com/ngm/ 0204/feature5/index.html |
| ⇒ Discovering Lewis and Clark | //www.lewis-clark.org |
| ⇒ Lewis & Clark—Mapping the West | //www.edgate.com/lewisandclark/ |
| ⇒ Ken Burns: Lewis & Clark: The Journey of the Corps of Dicovery | Video—240 minutes<br>Order from PBS |
| ⇒ Journals of Lewis & Clark by Meriwether Lewis, et. al. | Mariner Books; ISBN: 0395859964; Revised edition (April 30, 1997) |
| ⇒ Lewis & Clark: Voyage of Discovery by Stephen Ambrose, Sam Abell | National Geographic Society; ISBN:0792264738; bicentennial edition (March 2002) |

***Other Resources:***

Library resources on Lewis and Clark

**Activity:**

Have the students create a virtual tour for others designed to follow the trail of Lewis and Clark. The tour should be a guided list of web addresses with hints for each site about items not to miss.

Include a peer assessment component half-way through the work time to help insure that students are progressing adequately.

Allow time for student sharing about the various virtual tours.

Joanne J. Troutner

# Traveling Lewis and Clark's Trail Project

Your role as a tour guide group is to accomplish the following:

⇒ Use the Internet sites provided as your starting point. Also research other materials in the library media center. Pick one place to visit from each state.

⇒ Use Google (www.google.com) as your search engine to find other sites you may want to visit. Use the Virtual Tour chart to help you organize your information.

⇒ After you have decided on the sites for the virtual tour, begin work on the hint sheet for each site. Consider what things you want the viewers to gather or learn at each site. You will want to include at least two things the viewer needs to find or questions to be answered. You are welcome to do more. Focus on what the viewer will find interesting or what will help the viewer understand the exploration done by Lewis and Clark. Use the Hint Sheet chart to help you organize your information for this task.

**Assessment Ideas:**

⇒ Have teachers and/or students who are studying Lewis and Clark take the virtual tour and critique it.

⇒ Use the sample assessment rubric as a start for developing your own rubric.

⇒ Self evaluation questions—

1. How will I know I have done my personal best on this project?
2. Did I select the best resources for finding the information I needed?
3. Did I use the best methods to locate the information?
4. Did I work as a productive member of my group?
5. What could I have done to make the project experience better?

## Virtual Tour Planning Sheet

List the major topics/places your group needs to cover in the tour.

1.

2.

3.

4.

5.

6.

Brainstorm a list of search terms your group needs to use.

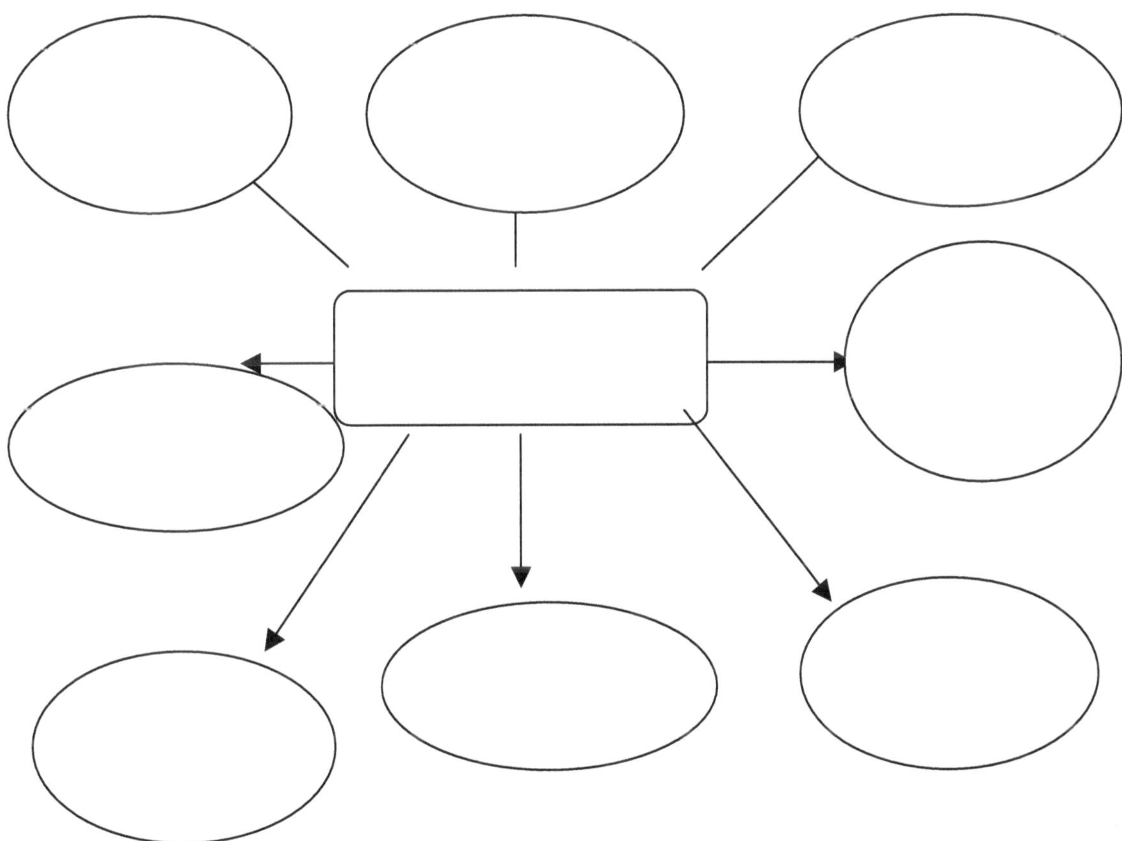

# Virtual Tour Chart

| Site | Address | Reason(s) to Include on Tour |
|---|---|---|
| | | |
| | | |
| | | |
| | | |
| | | |

# Hint Sheet Chart

| Site | Address | What Not to Miss/ Question to Answer/ Information to Find |
|---|---|---|
| | | |
| | | |
| | | |
| | | |
| | | |

# WWW Virtual Field Trip Sites

| ➢ Cathedral Tours | //www.newyorkcarver.com/cathedrallinks.htm |
|---|---|

Superb set of links for tours of cathedrals built during the Middle Ages

| ➢ Virtual Museums | //www.icom.org/vlmp/ |
|---|---|

Most complete list of museums with World Wide Web sites. Be sure to look at the Selected Virtual Exhibits section.

| ➢ Smithsonian Web Site | //www.si.edu/ |
|---|---|

The homepage for the vast collection of information stored at the Smithsonian web site. Notice the search button on the homepage.

| ➢ Grand Canyon | //www.kaibab.org/ |
|---|---|

Lots of visuals on this virtual trip throughout the Grand Canyon

| ➢ Expo Ticket Office | //www.ibiblio.org/expo/ticket_office.html |
|---|---|

Great virtual museum tours of several sites including the Vatican

| ➢ The Seven Wonders of the Ancient World | //ce.eng.usf.edu/pharos/wonders/ |
|---|---|

Excellent virtual tour of these ancient sites and history

| ➢ Tibet: A Virtual Field Trip | //jan.ucc.nau.edu/~wittke/Tibet/Tibet.html |
|---|---|

A delightful visual and educational look at this remote country

| ➢ Virtual Tour of Plimouth Plantation | //pilgrims.net/plimothplantation/vtour/index.htm |
|---|---|

Well designed tour of the original Plymouth colony

| ➢ Virtual Field Trips of Hawaii | //satftp.soest.hawaii.edu/space/hawaii/virtual.field.trips.html |
|---|---|

Field trip was devised from aerial views taken from a NASA plane

| ➢ Bosnian Virtual Fieldtrip | //monarch.gsu.edu/jcrampton/bosnia/ |
|---|---|

Very realistic field trip to Bosnia, which is updated occasionally

| ➢ National Park Service Homepage | //www.nps.gov/ |
|---|---|

A wonderful variety of information—be sure to visit the links to the past

| ➢ Harpers Ferry NHP Virtual Visitor Center | //www.nps.gov/hafe/home.htm |
|---|---|

Entryway to a wonderful virtual tour of this historic site

| ➢ Aboard the Underground Railroad | //www.cr.nps.gov/nr/travel/ underground/ |
|---|---|

A wonderful virtual tour of places on the National Park Service's National Register and the Underground Railroad route

| ➢ Visit Chicago | //www.cr.nps.gov/nr/travel/chicago/ chintro.htm |
|---|---|

A travel itinerary of historic places on the National Register in Chicago

| ➢ Expeditions | //www.discovery.com/guides/ expedition/expedition.html |
|---|---|

Changing list of excellent virtual trips from the Discovery Channel

| ➢ Monticello | //www.monticello.org/ |
|---|---|

Good tour of the home of Thomas Jefferson also check the lesson plans link

| ➢ Tour of Egypt | //www.memst.edu/egypt/main.html |
|---|---|

Visit the pyramids and other sites of the country

| ➢ Excite Travel | //travel.excite.com |
|---|---|

Wonderful site for gathering current travel information for students developing their own virtual field trips

| ➢ Tour of George Washington's Mount Vernon | //www.mountvernon.org |
|---|---|

A well done virtual tour with information on various artifacts found at the mansion.

| ➢ Machu Picchu, Peru Virtual Tour | //www.shastahome.com/machu-picchu/guide.html |
|---|---|

Well documented trip and reference information on the Incas

| ➢ Tour the Tower of London | //www.camelotintl.com/tower_site/tour/ index.html |
|---|---|

Completely narrated tour full of historical information

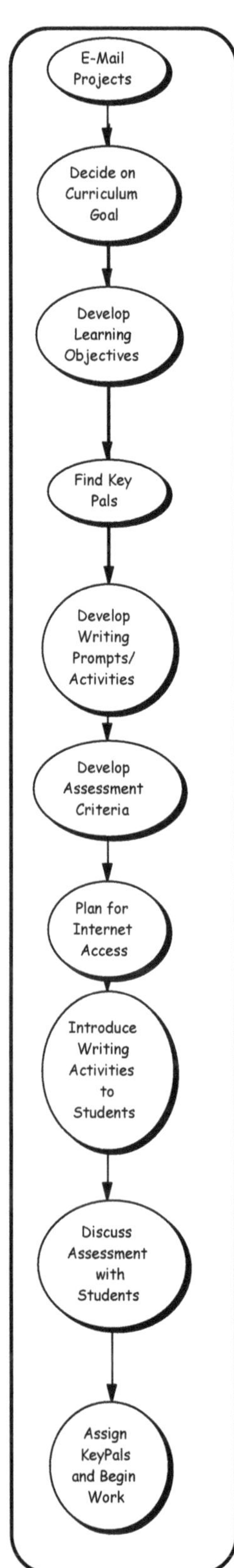


# Developing an E-Mail Project

Why use E-Mail Projects?

- ✓ Provide students with an audience for writing
- ✓ Provide students with a reason for research
- ✓ Provide practice on information gathering strategies
- ✓ Provide practice in becoming independent information seekers
- ✓ Provide opportunities to broaden point of view

Assessment Ideas—

- ✓ Simply grade the writing in the e-mail exchanges
- ✓ Develop a scoring rubric to track the research needed for the e-mail responses
- ✓ How will you know students have reached the learning objectives when you see it?

Classroom Management Tips—

- ✓ Review AUP and netiquette expectations
- ✓ Provide file naming conventions and file type information
- ✓ Keep list of student keypals and e-mail addresses used
- ✓ Provide clear expectations

# E-Mail Projects

***Planning Questions—***

- What is the curriculum goal of the project?
- Does the district or your school have an AUP for students to sign? What does the AUP say about e-mail use by students?
- Will students have their own e-mail accounts or be using a group account?
- What type of Internet access will your students have?
- How often can e-mail be sent or checked?
- Do you want to notify parents of your curriculum based e-mail project?
- How will you review student safety and netiquette with your students?
- How will you assess student performance?
- What timeline do you have in mind?
- Are there homework assignments, which both classes can do?

## What Will I Write?

- Include basic information about your life—school activities, pets, favorite foods, movies seen, career plans.
- What historical areas/parks are in your hometown?
- Visit the Census Bureau's website, //www.census.gov/, and compare and contrast the statistics of both communities.
- Write a collaborative story between you and your key pal.
- Read the same short story or book and compare your thoughts.
- Talk about local election issues.

- Discuss local community issues like a curfew, availability of jobs, or places to hang out.

- Visit the Filamentality Ideas webpage at //www.kn.pacbell.com/wired/fil/fr_pick_links.html for writing ideas.

## Sites for Finding Keypals—

| | |
|---|---|
| ePals Classroom Exchange | //www.epals.com/ |
| | |
| Keypals Club | //www.teaching.com/keypals/ |
| | |
| Intercultural E-Mail Classroom Connections | //www.teaching.com/IECC/ |
| | |
| Kidspace Connection | //www.ks-connection.org/ |

## Ask An Expert Sites—

| | |
|---|---|
| Ask An Expert Page | //www.k12science.org/askanexpert.html |
| | |
| Pitsco Ask An Expert | //www.askanexpert.com/ |

Visit these sites for more ideas and technical help—

| | |
|---|---|
| The Electronic Emissary | //emissary.ots.utexas.edu/emissary/index.html |
| | |
| Mystery from History | //www.indiana.edu/~leeehman/ mystery.pdf |

## Assessment Ideas—

- What are the curriculum goals of the project?

- What skills do you want students to practice?

- What student performance expectations do you have?

- Will you include a computer use component?

- What other things are important in this project?

**Classroom Management Tips—**

- Review AUP and netiquette expectations often.
- Provide student assessment process when the project is assigned.
- Provide file naming conventions and file type information if necessary.
- Keep list of student keypals and e-mail addresses used.

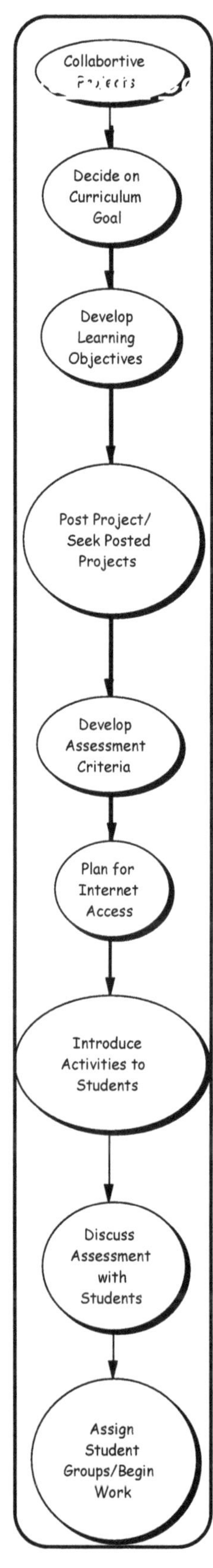


# Developing Collaborative Projects

Why use Collaborative Projects?

- ✓ Provide students with an audience for writing
- ✓ Provide students with a reason for research
- ✓ Provide practice on interpreting information
- ✓ Provide practice in becoming independent information seekers
- ✓ Provide opportunities to work as a team

Assessment Ideas—

- ✓ Simply grade the results of the project
- ✓ Develop a scoring rubric to track the research needed for the e-mail responses
- ✓ How will you know students have reached the learning objectives when you see it?

Classroom Management Tips—

- ✓ Review AUP and netiquette expectations
- ✓ Provide file naming conventions and file type information
- ✓ Keep list of student keypals and e-mail addresses used
- ✓ Provide clear expectations
- ✓ Keep task list and progress posted prominently in the classroom

# Collaborative Projects

**Planning Questions—**

- What is the curriculum goal of the project?
- Will the project involve data collection and analysis, online research, student publications, virtual adventures, and/or audio and video conferencing?
- Does the district or your school have an AUP for students to sign? What does the AUP say about e-mail use by students?
- Will students have their own e-mail accounts or be using a group account?
- What type of Internet access will your students have?
- How often can e-mail be sent or checked?
- Do you want to notify parents of your curriculum based collaborative project?
- What additional equipment is needed for the data collection in your project?
- How will you review student safety and netiquette with your students?
- How will you assess student performance?
- What timeline do you have in mind?
- Are there homework assignments, which both classes can do?
- How will registration be handled?
- What number of participants can you handle?

Check the Learning Center for Collaborative Projects at //www.globalschoolnet.org/center/index.html

**Sites for Finding & Advertising Collaborative Projects—**

| | |
|---|---|
| NickNacks | //telecollaborate.net/ |
| | |
| Online Projects | //www.att.com/learningnetwork/ teachers/projects.html |
| | |
| Learning Space Project List | //www.learningspace.org/connect/ projects.html |
| | |
| KidLink Network | //www.kidlink.org/KIDPROJ/ projects.html |
| | |
| Houghton Mifflin Project Center | //www.eduplace.com/projects/ index.html |
| | |
| TEAMS Classroom Projects | //teams.lacoe.edu/documentation/ projects/projects.html |

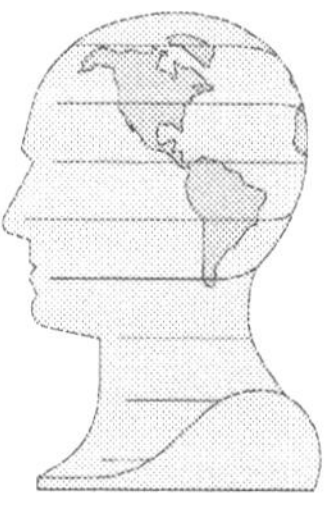

Read the article "*Using the Internet to Take a Field Trip and Encourage Writing*" at The Global Schoolhouse site, //www.techlearning.com/db_area/archives/WCE/archives/miracola3.htm

Check out the excellent staff development activity on "*Integrating the Internet into the Curriculum Creating Successful Internet Projects*" at //205.146.39.13/linktuts/intemain.htm.

***Classroom Management Tips***

- Review AUP and netiquette expectations often.
- Provide student assessment process when the project is assigned.
- Provide file naming conventions and file type information if necessary.
- Check student progress often.
- Keep lists of tasks and progress posted on the bulletin and prominently around the classroom.

## Assessment Ideas—

- What are the curriculum goals of the project?
- What skills do you want students to practice?
- What student performance expectations do you have?
- Will you include a computer use component?
- How will you assess non-computer activities?
- What other things are important in this project?

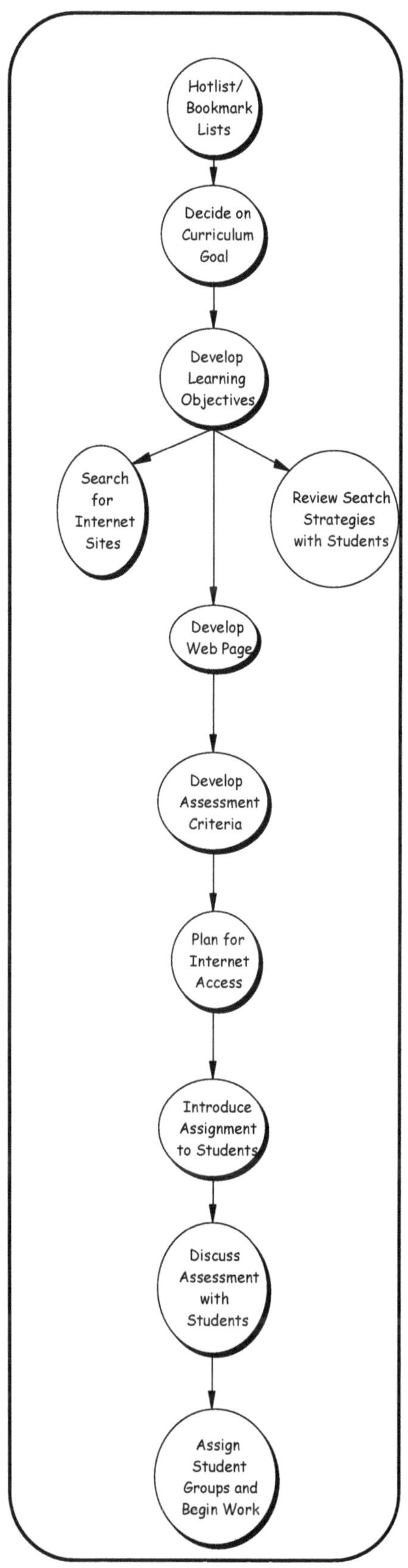


# Developing a Hotlist/Bookmark List

Why use Hotlists or Bookmark Lists?

- ✓ Provide structure for Internet activity
- ✓ Allow students to focus on gathering information from good Internet sites
- ✓ Provide practice on information gathering strategies
- ✓ Provide practice in becoming independent information seekers
- ✓ Maximize classroom time
- ✓ Provide students practice in searching and developing simple web pages

Assessment Ideas—

- ✓ Simply grade the product assigned
- ✓ Have students evaluate the sites selected
- ✓ How will you know students have reached the learning objectives when you see it?

Classroom Management Tips—

- ✓ Provide an example for student project
- ✓ Provide clear expectations
- ✓ Have students work in groups

# Hotlist Project

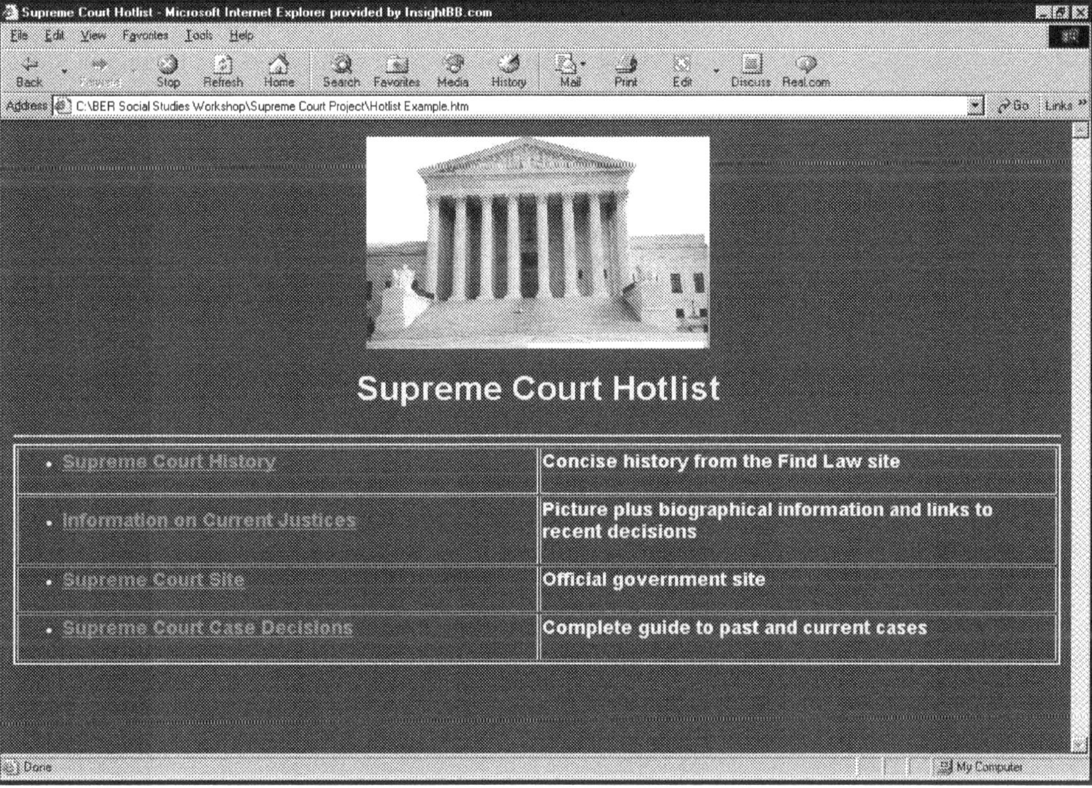


- ✓ Select a topic from the list provided. You will be exploring this topic throughout the semester.
- ✓ Your first project is to develop a Hotlist of at least four Internet sites related to your topic.
- ✓ Brainstorm a number of search terms. Remember that you may want to use phrases as well as "+" and "-" signs to narrow your search.
- ✓ Print your search results. Then highlight the first 10 sites you will visit in your search for the information, which best represents your topic. (You will need to hand in your search printout as part of your hotlist project.)
- ✓ After you select your sites, write your annotations. Also, you need to turn in an explanation of why you chose each site as the best 4 – 5 sites to represent your topic.
- ✓ Finally produce your web page, which contains your hotlist. Reference the example above as you create your own web page.

## Student Sample—Hotlist

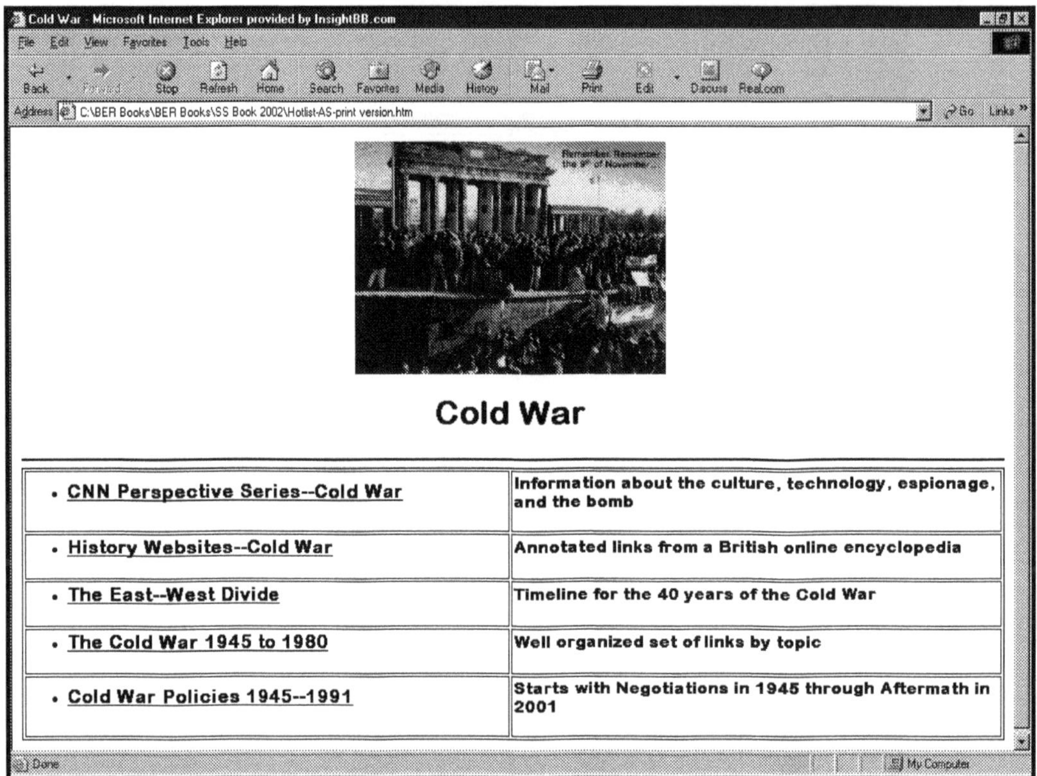

Cold War

| | |
|---|---|
| • CNN Perspective Series--Cold War | Information about the culture, technology, espionage, and the bomb |
| • History Websites--Cold War | Annotated links from a British online encyclopedia |
| • The East--West Divide | Timeline for the 40 years of the Cold War |
| • The Cold War 1945 to 1980 | Well organized set of links by topic |
| • Cold War Policies 1945--1991 | Starts with Negotiations in 1945 through Aftermath in 2001 |

I used the search terms “Cold War” + “world history”.

From the search results or from links found at a site listed by the search engine, I chose the five sites above.

I selected the CNN site because CNN is a reputable news organization and the site contained a variety of topics.

I chose the History Websites site because it provided another point of view. The source is from the United Kingdom.

I chose the East-West Divide because U.S. News and World Report is a good print news source and the timeline is well annotated.

I selected the last two sites because they provided a broad look at the Cold War and led to many other sites.

The hotlist webpage is stored in my home directory on the building network—H:\A...........

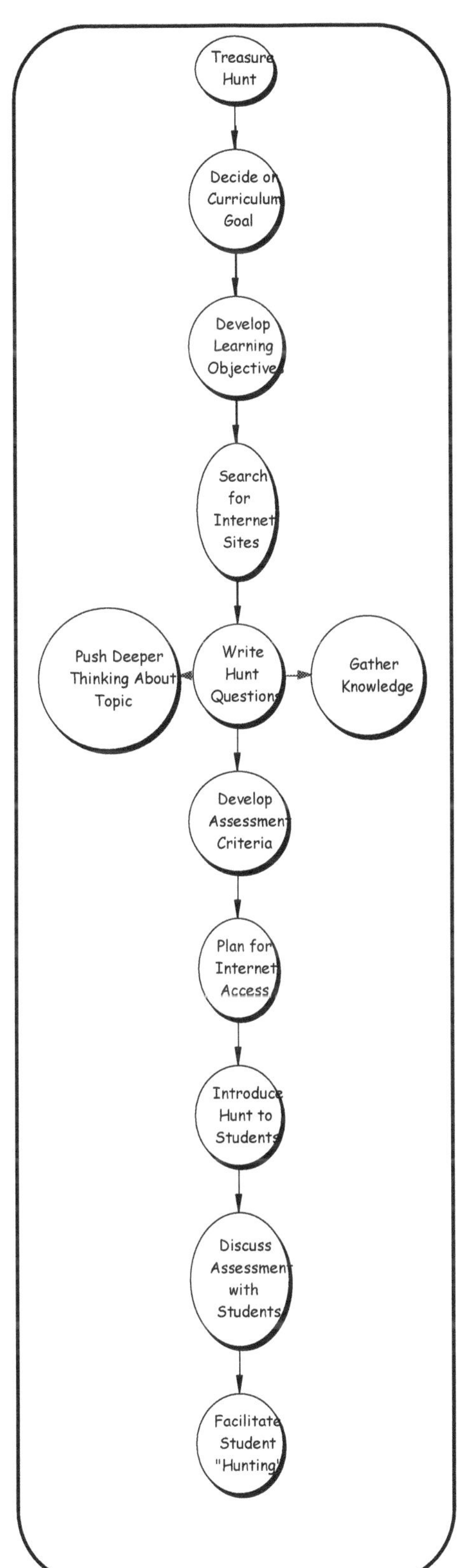


# Developing a Scavenger Hunt

Why use Scavenger Hunts?

- ✓ Gather information on a topic
- ✓ Spark student interest in a topic
- ✓ Provide practice on information gathering strategies
- ✓ Provide practice in becoming independent information seekers
- ✓ Provide practice in higher level thinking skills

Assessment Ideas—

- ✓ Simply grade the answers to questions
- ✓ Have students write a thinking response to one or two questions and assess that
- ✓ How will you know students have reached the learning objectives when you see it?

Classroom Management Tips—

- ✓ Provide bookmarks or simple web page with sites to use
- ✓ Provide clear expectations

Joanne J. Troutner

# Connecticut Yankee Scavenger Hunt

Begin your search with the Mark Twain site at //marktwain.about.com/cs/ twainmark/

- *Be sure to explain the thought process used when finding each answer.*

1. Find exhibits of advertising used when Connecticut Yankee was first published. Name two early 1890's publications, which contain these ads.

2. Locate a review of Connecticut Yankee published in Harpers magazine by W.D. Howells.

3. Locate the mural by E.A. Abbey done for the Boston Public Library on "The Achievement of the Grail."

4. Find a picture of Merlin done in the 19th century.

5. How many versions of Connecticut Yankee were done on film prior to 1940? List the years and the stars if available.

6. Where can you find a brief look at some of the shields used in the Arthurian legends?

7. What is the earliest reference to Arthur? Verify this information with a print resource.

8. Who was Sir Kay? What was on his shield?

9. Where can you find more information on the recent movie "First Knight?"

# Scavenger Hunt Project

- ✓ Your second project is to develop a scavenger hunt based on the sites you selected for your Hotlist.
- ✓ Visit each site on your webpage.
- ✓ Develop at least two questions for each site you have selected.
- ✓ Include in each question a link to the site where the person will find the answer to your question.
- ✓ For at least two questions include having the user write out his/her thought process for finding the answer.
- ✓ Think carefully about what information you want people to know about your topic.
- ✓ Craft a "Big Question" which will require the user to look at your topic in a broader, more thought provoking context.
- ✓ Consider the following examples of questions—

  When the Supreme Court started in 1790, what were the duties of the Chief Justice? (//supreme.lp.findlaw.com/supreme_court/supcthist.html)

  (Include space for the user to type the answers)

  Where did current Supreme Court Justice Antonin Scalia receive his A.B. degree? What is the most recent decision written by Justice Scalia? How did you navigate through the website to find the answers to these questions? (//supct.law.cornell.edu/supct/justices/scalia.bio.html)

  If you want to hear an oral argument of the Supreme Court, when could you do this? (//www.supremecourtus.gov/)

After gathering the answers to the above questions, reflect on your knowledge of the Supreme Court. Why is it important to have a Supreme Court? What are the 3 – 5 main concepts that a new voter should know about the Supreme Court?

Joanne J. Troutner

# Cold War Scavenger Hunt

- You can type your answers after each question. Simply put the cursor one line under the question and start typing.

- Remember to save the file with the filename ColdWarScavengerxx where xx are your initials.

1. Examine the "Alternate History" choices under the Technology link. Which one is the most plausible to you? Why? (//www.cnn.com/SPECIALS/cold.war/)

2. What were the three tools of the trade in espionage during the Cold War? In addition to answering the question, explain how you found the answer. (//www.cnn.com/SPECIALS/cold.war/)

3. Explore the link on McCarthyism. What as the HUCA? Who and what were the Hollywood 10? (//www.spartacus.schoolnet.co.uk/REVhistoryCOLD3.htm)

4. Read at least two of the oral histories on the Cuban Missile Crisis. What emotions do you think these people felt? (//www.spartacus.schoolnet.co.uk/REVhistoryCOLD3.htm)

5. When was the Warsaw Pact signed?
(http://www.usnews.com/usnews/news/991018/timeline.htm)

6. What are four crises that occurred during the Cold War?
(http://www.historylearningsite.co.uk/coldwar.htm)

7. What did the UN gain and lose during the Korean War?
(http://www.historylearningsite.co.uk/coldwar.htm)

8. Who is Konrad Adenauer? What was his role in the Cold War?
(//www.cnn.com/SPECIALS/cold.war/)

9. Read JFK's letter on "Preparing for Doomsday." If you were a high school student during this time period, how would you feel?
(//www.cnn.com/SPECIALS/cold.war/)

***Big Question—***

Pick the five most important events to take place during the Cold War time period. Why did you chose these events?

Joanne J. Troutner

# Learning About Tornadoes

⇒ Audience: Middle or high school students

⇒ Uses: Gather current scientific information
Learn to use Internet as a reference tool
Serve as a model for lessons on other weather phenomena

⇒ Curriculum Areas: Science

**The Tornado Project Online**

//www.tornadoproject.com/

*This site contains superb information on many facets of tornadoes. Current information, myths, history, the Fujita scale, links to other sites, and more are easily accessible.*

✎ Use an Internet Hunt to have students gather information

✎ Develop a set of safety guidelines for elementary students. Publish a pamphlet with the guidelines.

✎ Do a Powerpoint presentation on tornado history.

✎ Develop a Powerpoint presentation or a web page on what causes tornadoes. Be sure the materials can be used by 5th graders.

✎ Decide what information should be included for a 4th grade science lesson on tornadoes. Develop the lesson and present it.

## *Assessment Ideas*

✎ Use scoring rubrics for the presentations, which include criteria for content, presentation—oral and visual, design, and cooperative learning if applicable.

✎ Have a safety professional critique the tornado safety guideline publication.

✎ Have current 4th graders and 4th grade teachers critique the tornado lesson.

# Tornado Information Internet Hunt

***Be sure to include the methods and thinking you used to gather your information and answers.***

1. In April 1996, a tornado touched down at Fort Smith, Arkansas. What was the exact date and what was the damage?

2. The southwest corner of a basement is the safest location during a tornado—true or false? Site your source.

3. What state has the largest number of tornadoes? What state has the most killer tornadoes?

4. What is the Fujita Scale? Find a "traditional" reference source that backs up the information you find on the Internet.

5. What wind speeds cause moving cars to be blown off the road? What is the Fujita rating for this category of tornado?

6. Describe a tornado which took place in 1896.

7. Find information on tornado safety from two sites. Does the information agree?

8. What are waterspouts?

9. Find a description of a tornado and a closeup view graphic from USA Today.

10. Find a CNN news story on tornadoes.

Joanne J. Troutner

# WebQuest and Learning with the Internet

⇒ The WebQuest Page
//webquest.sdsu.edu/webquest.html

⇒ Building Blocks of a WebQuest
//projects.edtech.sandi.net/staffdev/buildingblocks/p-index.htm

⇒ A Strategy for Scaffolding Higher Level Learning
//webquest.sdsu.edu/necc98.htm

⇒ Tom March - Learning with the World
//www.ozline.com/learning/workshop.html

⇒ Web & Flow, by Tom March
//www.ozline.com/web-and-flow/in-service.html

⇒ Example WebQuests compiled by Bernie Dodge
//webquest.sdsu.edu/matrix.html

⇒ Wired Learning in the Classroom & Library
//www.kn.pacbell.com/wired/wired.html

⇒ Blue Web'n Applications
//www.kn.pacbell.com/wired/bluewebn/

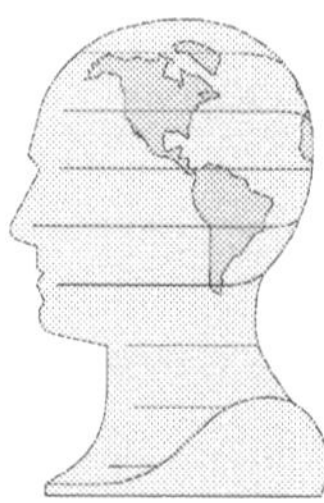

Take time to read the articles by Tom March at his web site on using the Internet as a learning tool and the excellent article on developing rubrics Nancy Pickett.

| | |
|---|---|
| "What's on the Web?" | //www.ozline.com/learning/webtypes.html |
| "Working the Web for Education" | //www.ozline.com/learning/theory.html |
| "Creating Rubrics" | //webquest.sdsu.edu/rubrics/weblessons.htm |

# What Is A WebQuest?

A WebQuest is a wonderful form of project based learning. The activity provides a structured learning environment. Students are provided with a well defined task, detailed instructions, the appropriate resources, and a scoring rubric. The goal is for the students to spend their energies developing the project.

Each WebQuest contains the following sections—

**Introduction**—This should be a short paragraph designed to motivate and hook the student. This will introduce the activity and provide the Essential or Guiding Question which the activity is centered around.

**Task**—This describes the actual project or task in a concise manner. Details are provided in a later section.

**Process**—This explains the task in detail. A step-by-step description should be supplied for the students. Provide guidance on how the information is to be gathered and structured. Resources are also listed in this section.

**Evaluation**—This contains the complete scoring rubric or evaluation process in detail.

**Conclusion**—This summarizes the task and asks some rhetorical or thought provoking questions about the activity/concept.

A great way to learn about WebQuests is to complete the WebQuest on WebQuests for your grade levels. This can be found at //webquest.sdsu.edu/materials.htm.

Remember the purpose of WebQuests is to provide students with practice in higher level thinking. Be sure you have an ample amount of higher level tasks. Consider using these words from Bloom's Taxonomy to help as you examine already developed WebQuests or craft your own.

- ✏ Analysis—analyze, separate, order, explain, connect, classify, arrange, divide, compare, select, explain, infer
- ✏ Synthesis—combine, integrate, modify, rearrange, substitute, plan, create, design, invent, compose, formulate, prepare, generalize, rewrite
- ✏ Evaluation—assess, decide, rank, grade, test, measure, recommend, convince, select, judge, explain, discriminate, support, conclude, compare, summarize

Joanne J. Troutner

# Hall of Fame Project

**Objectives:**

⇒ Technology — to use search engines to gather sites for a complex project
to access specific sites and use them as the starting place for gathering information

⇒ Core Curriculum — to practice presentation developing skills
to practice communications skills—oral and written
to develop visual presentations
to learn about famous people in the areas of literature, social studies, science, and math
to develop a process leading to a final event

⇒ Research/Reference — to gather information needed for a complex project
to disseminate information in various forms

**Internet Sources:**

Various Internet search engines which should reveal Internet sites dealing with the famous people selected by the students for the Hall of Fame

**Other Resources:**

Print and non-print biographical information sources

**Activity:**

Have the students create a Hall of Fame exhibit, which details the life and works of famous people in the areas of literature, social studies, science, and math. Students should work in cooperative groups with one group member focusing on each curriculum area. The Hall of Fame exhibit may be a Powerpoint slide show or a series of web pages.

Include a peer assessment component half-way through the work time to help insure that students are progressing adequately.

Allow time for student sharing of the various exhibits. Consider providing the students with an audience outside of their classmates.

**Assessment Ideas:**

Have teachers representing each subject area visit the exhibit and critique it.

Use the sample assessment rubric as a start for developing your own rubric.

# Hall of Fame Project

Your role as a curator for a Hall of Fame includes accomplishing the following:

1. Decide which four people will be in your group's Hall of Fame. Remember to include a person representing literature, social studies, science, and math.
2. Start your research by visiting the library media center and using your favorite search engine to gather information on the person you are going to represent.
3. Meet as a group to review your progress and share information on your individual person. Decide which pieces of information your group will include on each person in the Hall of Fame.
4. Decide what format your group will use to present the Hall of Fame exhibit.
5. Gather additional research and begin to work on a draft of your part of the exhibit.
6. As a group assess your progress and see what other information or help you need.
7. Complete your first draft of the exhibit and critique it as group.
8. Revise your exhibit based on your peer assessment.
9. Practice presenting your exhibit to an audience. Develop any handouts or print material you want the attendees to have when they visit your exhibit.
10. Test your equipment and have a backup presentation plan.

## Hall of Fame Planning Sheet

List the people your group is including the exhibit.

Literature—

Social Studies—

Science—

Math—

Brainstorm a list references and search terms your group needs to use.

## Hall of Fame Planning Chart

| Person | Info to Include | Resources |
|---|---|---|
| | | |
| | | |
| | | |
| | | |

## Hint Sheet Chart

| Exhibit Location | What Not to Miss/ Question to Answer/ Information to Find |
|---|---|
| | |
| | |
| | |
| | |

## Presentation Planning Chart

| Topic | Who |
| --- | --- |
| | |
| | |
| | |
| | |
| | |

# Discovering Canada

| ⇒ Audience: | Middle school and high school students |
|---|---|

| ⇒ Curriculum Area: | Geography<br><br>Social Studies |
|---|---|

| ⇒ NCSS Strands | (1) Culture<br><br>(3) People, Places, and Environments |
|---|---|

✏ Divide the class into groups. Have each group pick from or assign the following topics:

| Landforms | Water Systems | Resources |
|---|---|---|
| | | |
| Climates | Vegetation | Population Patterns |
| | | |
| History & Government | Cultures & Lifestyles | Environment |
| | | |
| Agriculture | Manufacturing & Service | Transportation & Communications |

✏ Each group is to develop 2 – 3 PowerPoint slides to explain their topic.

✏ Assign one student to be the PowerPoint engineer. This student will be responsible for collecting the group slides and putting them together into one PowerPoint presentation.

✏ Provide students with guidelines on what to include for each topic.

✏ Provide scoring rubric or assessment criteria as assignment is given.

# Developing an Overview

Answer these questions before you begin developing your PowerPoint slides.

✓ What are the important parts of my topic? What does my audience already know about Canada? What geographic terms do I need to include?

✓ What sources will I use to find appropriate graphics? Where will I store these graphics?

✓ What file name should we use for our work? Where are we to store our work?

✓ What resources will you use to gather your information? What is the location of these resources?

# Slide Show Planning Sheet

Select the graphics you wish to use in your slides. Use the chart to keep track of images you will use.

| Picture | Source | Where Stored |
|---|---|---|
| | | |
| | | |
| | | |
| | | |
| | | |
| | | |
| | | |
| | | |

Use the assessment rubric to look at your slides and then make any changes you feel are needed.

# PowerPoint Planning Guide

Notes:

Notes:

Notes:

# Solar System

⇒ Audience: Middle school students

⇒ Uses: Provide current scientific information

Provide visuals not readily available from other science reference tools

⇒ Curriculum Areas: Science
Math
Language Arts

**Views of the Solar System**

//www.solarviews.com/ss.html

*This tour contains information on the Sun, planets, moons, asteroids, comets, and meteoroids found in our solar system. Over 200 pages of information, 970 illustrations, and 840 MB of information are available at this address.*

✏ Divide the class into groups. Have each group pick one of the links on the homepage. Then have the groups develop a similar set of web pages for elementary students.

✏ Develop a set of trading cards for each planet.

✏ Do research on Voyager 2 and share the results with your class.

✏ Write a description of a being that could survive on Saturn. Include information about how the being will survive in the atmosphere and the winds.

✏ How many moons does Saturn have?

✏ Write a news story telling about Saturn's rings. What new developments have been found?

✏ What is the radius of the moon Atlas in miles?

✏ Create a graphic which shows Saturn's moons and illustrates their sizes.

✏ When was the first moon discovered around Saturn? Who discovered it? Write an entry for a biographical dictionary on the discoverer.

✏ Create a slide show complete with music which tells the story of Saturn.

✏ Capture an image of Saturn. Then write a detailed description of it.

✏ What is synchronous rotation?

✏ What can you discover about Voyager 1?

✏ What is the Cassini Mission? Why is it important?

✏ Summarize the Voyager Saturn science information for use by a 4th grader.

✏ What is a magnetosphere? How did it effect Voyager?

✏ Write an editorial designed to convince your local politicians to support funding of the Cassini mission.

---

## Assessment Ideas

✏ Use the content and design evaluation sheets on the student developed web pages.

✏ Have a journalist or high school journalism students critique the news story about Saturn's ring and the editorial.

✏ Use scoring rubrics on the trading cards, research on Voyager 2, and a slide show on Saturn. The rubrics should cover the areas of design, content information, presentation—oral and visual, and cooperative learning if applicable.

# Trading Card Activity

Draw a paper mock-up of your trading card before you develop it. Ask the following questions.

1. Is the layout appealing?
2. What font or typestyle will you use?
3. What size type will you use?
4. Will you use bold, italics, or underline to emphasize any information?

Be sure your trading card includes the following:

◊ The name of the planet

◊ The name(s) of any moons

◊ The weather on the planet

◊ A picture of the planet

◊ The length of a day and a year on the planet

◊ The atmosphere on the planet

◊ The distance of the planet from the sun and from Earth if applicable

◊ Places where further information can be found

Joanne J. Troutner

# Writing an Editorial

Answer these questions before you begin writing.

- ✓ Who is your audience? What do you know about them? What uses do they make of information found on space missions?

- ✓ What factors about the Cassini Mission will appeal to your audience?

- ✓ What factors will be considered negative by your audience?

- ✓ How can you address the negatives? Can any of them be turned into a positive?

# Slide Show Planning Sheet

Select the planet you wish to use in your slide show. Use the chart to keep track of images you will use.

| Picture | Source | Where Stored |
| --- | --- | --- |
| | | |
| | | |
| | | |
| | | |
| | | |
| | | |
| | | |
| | | |
| | | |
| | | |
| | | |
| | | |
| | | |
| | | |
| | | |

Use the assessment rubric to look at your slide show and then make any changes you feel are needed.

# Journal Entry Template

- Who is writing the entry?
- How old is the person?
- What emotions does the author want to convey?
- What facts does the author want to convey?

# National Geographic Expedition

⇒ Audience: Middle and high school students
⇒ Uses: Expand knowledge of geography
Gather more information about the environment
Expand knowledge of history
⇒ Curriculum Areas: Social Studies and Science

**National Geographic Magazine** //www.nationalgeographic.com/media/ngm/9607/0026.html

✔ View the article on Parks in South Africa and compare it with the print version. Which is more effective? Why?

✔ Research the elephant. What other methods could be used to solve the elephant population problem? Develop an advertising campaign or a presentation to the person in charge of parks in South Africa.

✔ Develop a Powerpoint presentation which gives the background needed on elephants to help understand the plight of the parks.

✔ Develop your own "National Geographics" presentation about another animal found in South African parks.

✔ Look at the Silver Bank article on-line. Then research coral reefs. What things will salvage operators need to keep in mind as they do their work? Develop a set of web pages, Powerpoint slide, or a printed handbook with the proper procedures to help protect the coral reef.

✔ Assume you are a member of the expedition team responsible for developing a Smithsonian Institute exhibit on the treasures of the Concepcion. Use the daily report and features to develop the outline of the exhibit.

# Assessment Ideas

✔ Use scoring rubrics for the presentations and web pages, which include criteria for content, presentation—oral and visual, design, and cooperative learning if applicable.
✔ Present the alternative method for solving the elephant population problem to local zoo or animal experts.
✔ Have an oceanographer critique the suggestions for the salvage operators.

# Virtual Trip to Mammoth Cave
# Teacher's Notes

**Objectives:**

| | |
|---|---|
| ⇒ Technology | to access a specific site and use it as the starting place for gathering information |
| ⇒ Core Curriculum | to practice presentation developing skills<br>to develop visual presentation<br>to practice writing skills<br>to explore earth science concepts related to caves<br>to understand environmental concerns and solutions<br>to solve a community problem |
| ⇒ Research/Reference | to gather information needed for a complex project<br>to disseminate information in various forms |

**Internet Sources:**

The National Park Service site for Mammoth Cave
//www.nps.gov/maca/ and //www.nps.gov/maca/home.htm

**Other Resources:**

Library resources on environmental issues

**Activity:**

Decide which of the suggested activities students will complete. Assign the activities and schedule work time during class for the groups. Review the necessary presentation development skills.

Include a peer assessment component half-way through the work time to help insure that students are progressing adequately.

Allow time for student sharing about the various activities.

# Virtual Trip to Mammoth Cave

Use the National Park Service site as a starting place for information and for the virtual tour options. The address is //www.nps.gov/maca//. Use the Nature & Science link as a starting point. Then visit //www.nps.gov/maca/ExploringDeeper.html. Suggested activities could include the following:

- Explore the history of the park. Write a journal entry for a person who would have helped discover the cave and the park area.
- Access the cave life webpage on Mammoth Cave. Select one animal and develop a visual presentation suitable for a fellow classmate.
- Develop a trading card for each type of cave life. Make the information suitable for use by a younger student.
- What is topography? Write a definition that a younger student would understand.
- Describe how Mammoth Cave was formed. Include illustrations.
- What does the term "karst" mean? Develop a visual presentation on karst topography.
- What other national parks have caves? What are the similarities and differences in the ways these caves were formed?
- Develop a brochure describing a tour of Mammoth Cave designed for middle school earth science students.
- Develop a brochure describing a tour of Mammoth Cave designed for high school biology students.
- Explore the endangered species. Select two items. Develop a plan to make the environment at Mammoth Cave more friendly to these species.
- Write a letter to the editor to support your environmental plan.
- Investigate other national parks with caves. What environmental concerns do they have?

- Take the Tour of the Cave in 1844 found at the NPS web site. Write journal entries from the viewpoint of someone your age.

- What is a biosphere reserve? Can this be used as part of your environmental plan? Write a letter to your US senator asking that this program be enlarged.

## *Assessment Ideas*

- Have younger students use the trading cards to gather information.

- Use a scoring rubric on the visual presentation, the park brochures which includes areas for design, content, presentation—oral and visual, and cooperative learning if applicable.

- Test the letter to the editor on a series of adults.

- Have the local state conservation officer look at your environmental plan.

# Trading Card Activity

Draw a paper mock-up of your trading card before you develop it. Ask the following questions.

1. Is the layout appealing?
2. What font or typestyle will you use?
3. What size type will you use?
4. Will you use bold, italics, or underline to emphasize any information?

Be sure your trading card includes the following:

- The type of cave life
- The name of the animal
- The life cycle of the animal
- A picture of the animal
- The food eaten by the animal
- Places where further information can be found

# Environment Plan Worksheet

➔ What area(s) of the environment need improving for your species to survive?

➔ How can these changes be accomplished?

➔ Will these changes impact other species? If so, how? If not, explain why.

➔ Will these changes impact the park community and the surrounding local area? If so, how? If not, explain why.

➔ What is the financial impact of your plan?

# Journal Entry Template

- Who is writing the entry?

- How old is the person?

- What emotions does the author want to convey?

- What facts does the author want to convey?

# Brochure Development Worksheet

Your brochure is to be a tri-fold like most travel brochures.

Do a mock-up on paper first. Ask the following questions.

1. Is the layout appealing?
2. What font or typestyle will you use?
3. What size type will you use?
4. Will you use bold, italics, or underline to emphasize any information?

---

Be sure you include the following:

- ➔ Information about lodging
- ➔ Directions to the park
- ➔ Reasons why the target audience will want to visit
- ➔ Further contact information
- ➔ Appropriate visuals

# CNN Exploration

⇒ Audience: High school students

⇒ Uses: Provide access to current events

Provide information on a wide range of topics

Provide materials for critical thinking activities

⇒ Curriculum Areas: Social Studies
Language Arts

**CNN Interactive**

//www.cnn.com/

*This frequently updated site provides access to the wealth of news, video, and audio information available from the CNN newsroom.*

- Look at the full story of the current headline. Is it written in a factual or emotional style? What emotion do the visuals evoke? How would you change the story and visuals to make the story more factual and evoke less emotion?
- Take the News Quiz. Develop one of your own.
- Look at the World News section. Write an encyclopedia entry for one topic.
- Look at the digest of today's news. What picture do you get of the U.S. from this news digest? How would you suggest the digest be changed?
- Pick one story and rewrite it from another point of view.
- Do you detect any bias in the news stories? If so, give examples.
- Assume you had to choose what news to include in the digest. What would you choose?

- Design a CNN-type digest of news for your school.
- Look at the U.S. news. How will these events impact the other countries of the world?
- Watch the local news tonight. Write the plan for making a CNN digest for it.

## Assessment Ideas

- Have another student read the encyclopedia entry and critique it.
- Have journalists, news reporters, or students studying these careers critique the CNN digest plan, the school news cast, the activities related to bias, and the suggestions on changing the CNN digest for the day.
- Discuss the perception gained of the United States with students from another social studies class or a group of college students.
- 

# Investigating the Civil War

**Objectives:**

| | |
|---|---|
| ⇒ Core Curriculum | to practice presentation developing skills<br>to practice communications skills—oral and written<br>to develop visual presentations<br>to learn about the political climate before and during the Civil War<br>to learn about military strategy and battles during the Civil War<br>to learn about medicine and science during the time of the Civil War<br>to practice math computation<br>to develop a process leading to a final event |

| | |
|---|---|
| ⇒ Research/Reference | to gather information needed for a complex project<br>to evaluate information to see if it is credible<br>to disseminate information in various forms |

| | |
|---|---|
| ⇒ NCSS Strands | (2) Time, Continuity, and Change<br>(6) Power, Authority, and Governance |

**Internet Sources—**

Various Internet search engines, which should reveal some of the following sites

| | |
|---|---|
| United States Civil War | //www.us-civilwar.com/ |
| The Civil War Homepage | //www.civil-war.net/ |
| The American Civil War Homepage | //sunsite.utk.edu/civil-war// |
| Life Stories of Civil War Heroes | //www.geocities.com/Athens/Aegean/6732/ |
| Selected Civil War Photographs | //memory.loc.gov/ammem/cwphtml/cwphome.html |
| The American Civil War | //homepages.dsu.edu/jankej/civilwar/civilwar.htm |

**Other Resources:**

Library resources on the Civil War in the United States

**Activity:**

Have the students create museum exhibits detailing the politics in the US before and during the Civil War, military strategy and battles of the Civil War, as well as medicine and science during the Civil War. These exhibits can be web pages, PowerPoint slide shows, diorama type constructions, or any other format you choose. Each exhibit should include a printed exhibit guide.

Include a peer assessment component half-way through the work time to help insure that students are progressing adequately.

Allow time for student sharing of the various exhibits.

---

## ➢ Assessment Ideas—

- ✓ Use a scoring rubric for the web pages and PowerPoint projects
- ✓ Have a museum curator help with assessing the exhibits
- ✓ Check to see if there is a Civil War history organization in the community and enlist the members to help gauge the success of the student exhibits

---

Include a student performance component in the assessment.

Have students develop a timeline for getting the work done.

Be sure that file name standards are explained and used by the students.

# Investigating the Civil War Project

Your role as a museum exhibit creator for either the political issues before and during the Civil War, military strategy and battles of the Civil War, or medicine and science during the Civil War is to accomplish the following:

1. Brainstorm your search terms and plan your research strategy as a group BEFORE beginning to look for resources.

2. Divide up the terms and begin searching for those resources you want to recommend for your exhibit. Be sure to evaluate the information and make certain you feel it is creditable. Use the Museum Exhibit Planning Sheet and your knowledge about evaluating information to accomplish this task. *Be sure to include graphics where appropriate in your exhibit.*

3. After you have decided on the materials for the exhibit, begin work on the presentation your group will develop. Use the Presentation Planning Chart to help keep track of decisions and the Hint Sheet to develop the printed guide to your exhibit.

4. Now, assemble the pieces of your exhibit into a complete draft exhibit.

5. Do a trial visit of your exhibit and complete a peer assessment. Also consider having either fellow students, a teacher, or another adult look at the exhibit and provide you with feedback.

6. Refine/revise your exhibit.

7. See that handouts are copied, the necessary hardware is available, proper software is loaded, and have a backup copy of your exhibit.

---

***Assessment Ideas—***

- Have teachers and/or students who are studying the Civil War visit the exhibit and critique it.

- Use the sample assessment rubric as a start for developing your own rubric.

# Museum Exhibit Planning Sheet

★ List the major topics your group needs to cover in the exhibit.

1.

2.

3.

4.

5.

6.

★ Brainstorm a list of search terms your group needs to use.

# Museum Exhibit Chart

| Resource | Address/Location | Reason(s) to Include in the Exhibit |
|---|---|---|
| | | |
| | | |
| | | |
| | | |
| | | |

# Hint Sheet Chart

| Exhibit Location | What Not to Miss/ Question to Answer/ Information to Find |
|---|---|
| | |
| | |
| | |
| | |

Your final project consists of two parts.

Part I—

Develop an annotated bibliography of WebQuests related to your topic.

The annotations need to include the a brief description of the project to be developed, an estimate of the time required to complete the WebQuest, your opinion of how well the WebQuest covers the concepts of your topic, and your rating.

The rating scale is 1 – 5 with 5 being the highest and 1 being the lowest.

The bibliography entry needs to include the title of the WebQuest and the address where it can be found.

Part II—

Develop an overview of your topic.

Use PowerPoint to develop a presentation, which presents the following:

- the important people with a brief description of their role
- the important events with a description of how these events relate to the topic
- a timeline relating to the topic
- at least two questions which require the viewer to synthesize the information presented
- appropriate bibliographic citations

Develop your presentation using the storyboard sheets provided. Be prepared to turn in your storyboard sheets.

You will do an oral presentation with your PowerPoint creation as your visuals.

Your final project will be scored using the Final Project rubric.

# PowerPoint Planning Guide

Notes:

Notes:

Notes:

# Assessment

***How do you assess projects?***

⇒ Scoring rubrics

⇒ Peer assessment

⇒ Expert assessment

⇒ ?????

What is important in this project?

What do you want students to learn?

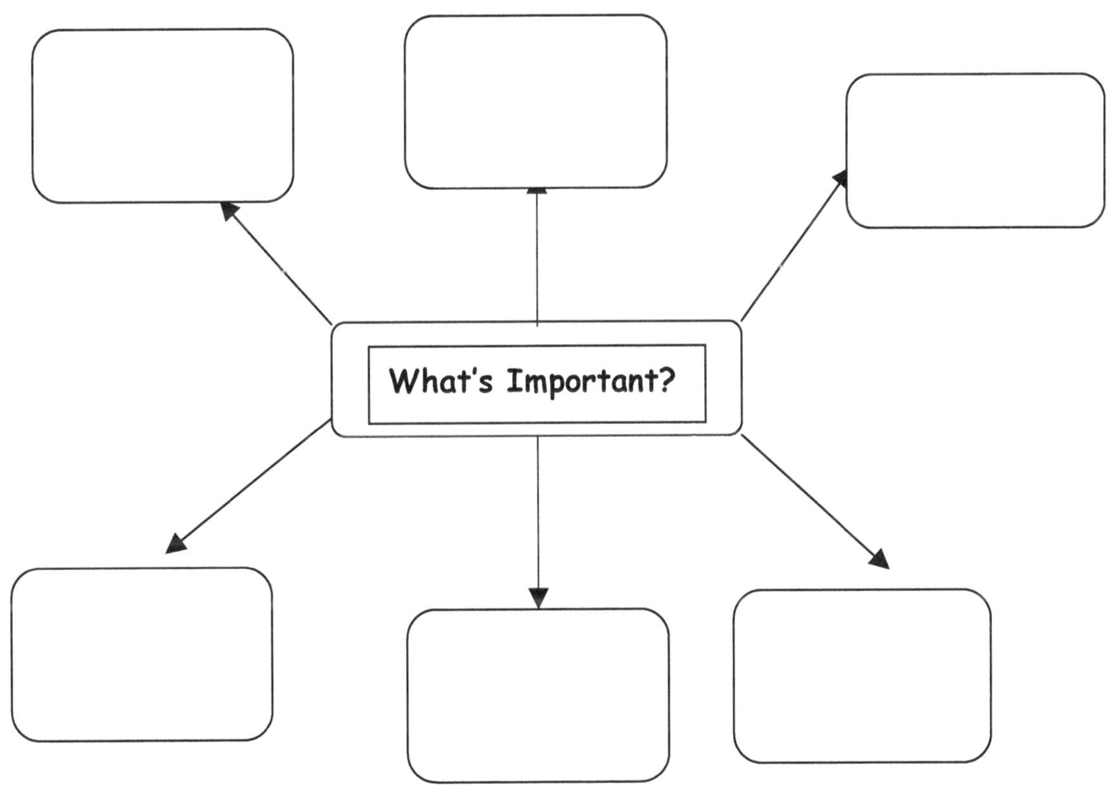

# Sample Assessment Rubric

## Assessment of Content

| | | | |
|---|---|---|---|
| • Topic covered adequately—enough details to cover concept event, or time period | 7 | 5 | 1 |
| • Logical progression of information | 7 | 5 | 1 |
| • Includes concrete examples related to the concept | 7 | 5 | 1 |
| • Introduction clearly states purpose | 7 | 5 | 1 |
| • Ideas/processes clear | 7 | 5 | 1 |
| • Demonstrates depth of knowledge | 7 | 5 | 1 |
| • Able to answer questions | 7 | 5 | 1 |

## Assessment of Research Skills

| | | | |
|---|---|---|---|
| • Uses Internet resources—are valid and reliable | 5 | 3 | 1 |
| • Uses varied resources—books, magazines, experts | 5 | 3 | 1 |
| • Has bibliography | 5 | 3 | 1 |
| • Cites sources | 5 | 3 | 1 |
| • Avoid plagiarism | 5 | 3 | 1 |

## Assessment of Oral Presentation

| | | | |
|---|---|---|---|
| • Good eye contact | 5 | 3 | 1 |
| • People at back of room can hear | 5 | 3 | 1 |
| • Demonstrated ease with topic | 5 | 3 | 1 |
| • Answers questions politely | 5 | 3 | 1 |
| • Smiles, shows enthusiasm in voice | 5 | 3 | 1 |
| • Visuals handled smoothly | 5 | 3 | 1 |
| • Doesn't read the entire visual | 5 | 3 | 1 |

## Assessment of Visual Presentation

| | | | |
|---|---|---|---|
| • Help explain concept | 5 | 3 | 1 |
| • Are large enough to be seen clearly at the back of the classroom | 5 | 3 | 1 |
| • Include appropriate graphics | 5 | 3 | 1 |
| • Graphics serve a purpose | 5 | 3 | 1 |
| • Visual transitions handled smoothly | 5 | 3 | 1 |
| • Pleasing color scheme/easy to read | 5 | 3 | 1 |
| • Lettering is easy to read and large enough | 5 | 3 | 1 |

## Assessment of Cooperative Learning Skills

| | | | |
|---|---|---|---|
| • Contributes ideas to group | 5 | 3 | 1 |
| • Willingness to contribute | 5 | 3 | 1 |
| • Contributes with written materials for the group project | 5 | 3 | 1 |
| • Meets deadlines | 5 | 3 | 1 |
| • Brings supplies | 5 | 3 | 1 |
| • No bickering or whining | 5 | 3 | 1 |
| • Ability to compromise | 5 | 3 | 1 |
| • Revise work as needed to fit group project | 5 | 3 | 1 |
| • Accepts constructive comments | 5 | 3 | 1 |
| • Ability to tactfully provide constructive comments | 5 | 3 | 1 |
| • Gives positive feedback to group | 5 | 3 | 1 |

Joanne J. Troutner

# Sample PowerPoint Assessment Rubric

## Assessment of Content

| | | | |
|---|---|---|---|
| • Topic covered adequately for beginning to intermediate Internet users | 7 | 5 | 1 |
| • Logical progression of information | 7 | 5 | 1 |
| • Includes concrete examples of how and when use the feature | 7 | 5 | 1 |
| • Introduction clearly states purpose | 7 | 5 | 1 |
| • Ideas/processes clear | 7 | 5 | 1 |
| • Demonstrates depth of knowledge | 7 | 5 | 1 |
| • Able to answer questions | 7 | 5 | 1 |

## Assessment of Research Skills

| | | | |
|---|---|---|---|
| • Uses Internet resources | 5 | 3 | 1 |
| • Uses varied resources—books, magazines, experts | 5 | 3 | 1 |
| • Has bibliography | 5 | 3 | 1 |
| • Cites sources | 5 | 3 | 1 |
| • Avoid plagiarism | 5 | 3 | 1 |

## Assessment of Visual Presentation

| | | | |
|---|---|---|---|
| • Help explain concept | 5 | 3 | 1 |
| • Are large enough to be seen clearly at the back of the classroom | 5 | 3 | 1 |
| • Include appropriate graphics | 5 | 3 | 1 |
| • Graphics serve a purpose | 5 | 3 | 1 |
| • Visual transitions handled smoothly | 5 | 3 | 1 |
| • Pleasing color scheme/easy to read | 5 | 3 | 1 |
| • Lettering is easy to read and large enough | 5 | 3 | 1 |

# Discovering Canada Assessment Rubric

## Assessment of Content

| | | | |
|---|---|---|---|
| • Topic covered adequately—includes appropriate geographic terms | 7 | 5 | 1 |
| • Logical progression of information | 7 | 5 | 1 |
| • Includes concrete examples of the concept | 7 | 5 | 1 |
| • Purpose is clear | 7 | 5 | 1 |
| • Ideas/processes clear | 7 | 5 | 1 |
| • Demonstrates depth of knowledge | 7 | 5 | 1 |
| • Able to answer questions | 7 | 5 | 1 |

## Assessment of Research Skills

| | | | |
|---|---|---|---|
| • Uses appropriate, reliable Internet resources | 5 | 3 | 1 |
| • Uses varied resources—books, magazines, experts | 5 | 3 | 1 |
| • Has bibliography and/or cites sources | 5 | 3 | 1 |
| • Shows ability to develop an overview | 5 | 3 | 1 |
| • Avoid plagiarism | 5 | 3 | 1 |

## Assessment of Visual Presentation

| | | | |
|---|---|---|---|
| • Help explain concept | 5 | 3 | 1 |
| • Are large enough to be seen clearly at the back of the classroom | 5 | 3 | 1 |
| • Include appropriate graphics | 5 | 3 | 1 |
| • Graphics serve a purpose | 5 | 3 | 1 |
| • Visual transitions handled smoothly | 5 | 3 | 1 |
| • Pleasing color scheme/easy to read | 5 | 3 | 1 |
| • Lettering is easy to read and large enough | 5 | 3 | 1 |

# Hotlist Project Rubric

## Assessment of Content

| | | | |
|---|---|---|---|
| • Sites selected relate to project content | 7 | 5 | 1 |
| • Sites selected provide a good range of information sources for selected audience | 7 | 5 | 1 |
| • Annotations provide enough information for user to make easy selection | 7 | 5 | 1 |
| • Sites selected are of appropriate reading level for target audience | 7 | 5 | 1 |
| • Sites selected are reliable and can be validated | 7 | 5 | 1 |
| • Site selection illustrates understanding of range of topic being covered | 7 | 5 | 1 |

## Assessment of Research Skills

| | | | |
|---|---|---|---|
| • Internet search shows knowledge of developing keyword searches | 7 | 5 | 1 |
| • Internet search shows knowledge of using phrases, include, and exclude options | 7 | 5 | 1 |
| • Printout of Internet search has between 10 – 15 sites highlighted for further investigation | 7 | 5 | 1 |
| • Site selection shows evidence of content evaluation | 7 | 5 | 1 |
| • Site selection shows evidence of design evaluation | 7 | 5 | 1 |

Comments:

# Scavenger Hunt Project Rubric

## Assessment of Content

| | | | |
|---|---|---|---|
| • Questions require the use of all sites | 7 | 5 | 1 |
| • Questions provide students option to explore the information found at each site | 7 | 5 | 1 |
| • Hunt includes directions to explain thought process for finding answers | 7 | 5 | 1 |
| • Questions combine to provide a thorough overview of the topic | 7 | 5 | 1 |
| • Questions are designed to help motivate user to explore the topic further | 7 | 5 | 1 |
| • "Big Question" requires students to analyze and synthesize the information found | 7 | 5 | 1 |

## Assessment of Construction Skills

| | | | |
|---|---|---|---|
| • Hunt is constructed with easy access to links for finding the answer | 7 | 5 | 1 |
| • User can easily add answers to the hunt after each question | 7 | 5 | 1 |
| • Questions are grammatically correct | 7 | 5 | 1 |

Comments:

Joanne J. Troutner

# *Final Project Assessment Rubric*

## Assessment of Content

| | | | |
|---|---|---|---|
| • Topic covered adequately—enough details to cover concept, event, or time period | 7 | 5 | 1 |
| • Logical progression of information | 7 | 5 | 1 |
| • Includes people involved in the topic—shows understanding of the people's roles | 7 | 5 | 1 |
| • Includes the main events of the topic/time period—shows understanding of the events | 7 | 5 | 1 |
| • Includes timeline with appropriate events listed | 7 | 5 | 1 |
| • Demonstrates depth of knowledge | 7 | 5 | 1 |
| • Able to answer questions | 7 | 5 | 1 |
| • Includes two thought provoking questions to provide the viewer with synthesis activity | 7 | 5 | 1 |
| • Thought provoking questions demonstrate knowledge of the topic | 7 | 5 | 1 |

## Assessment of Research Skills

| | | | |
|---|---|---|---|
| • Uses Internet resources | 5 | 3 | 1 |
| • Uses varied resources—books, magazines, experts | 5 | 3 | 1 |
| • Has bibliography | 5 | 3 | 1 |
| • Cites sources | 5 | 3 | 1 |
| • Avoid plagiarism | 5 | 3 | 1 |

## Assessment of Visual Presentation

| | | | |
|---|---|---|---|
| • Help explain concept | 5 | 3 | 1 |
| • Are large enough to be seen clearly at the back of the classroom | 5 | 3 | 1 |
| • Include appropriate graphics | 5 | 3 | 1 |

## Assessment of Visual Presentation—continued

| | | | |
|---|---|---|---|
| • Graphics serve a purpose | 5 | 3 | 1 |
| • Visual transitions handled smoothly | 5 | 3 | 1 |
| • Pleasing color scheme/easy to read | 5 | 3 | 1 |
| • Lettering is easy to read and large enough | 5 | 3 | 1 |

## Assessment of Oral Presentation

| | | | |
|---|---|---|---|
| • Good eye contact | 5 | 3 | 1 |
| • People at back of room can hear | 5 | 3 | 1 |
| • Demonstrated ease with topic | 5 | 3 | 1 |
| • Answers questions politely | 5 | 3 | 1 |
| • Smiles, shows enthusiasm in voice | 5 | 3 | 1 |
| • Visuals handled smoothly | 5 | 3 | 1 |
| • Doesn't read the entire visual | 5 | 3 | 1 |

Comments:

# Rubric

## Assessment of Content

| | | | |
|---|---|---|---|
| • | | | |
| • | | | |
| • | | | |
| • | | | |
| • | | | |
| • | | | |
| • | | | |

## Assessment of Research Skills

| | | | |
|---|---|---|---|
| • | | | |
| • | | | |
| • | | | |
| • | | | |
| • | | | |

## Assessment of Oral Presentation

| | | | |
|---|---|---|---|
| • | | | |
| • | | | |
| • | | | |
| • | | | |
| • | | | |
| • | | | |
| • | | | |

## Assessment of Visual Presentation

| | | | |
|---|---|---|---|
| • | | | |
| • | | | |
| • | | | |
| • | | | |
| • | | | |
| • | | | |
| • | | | |

## Assessment of Cooperative Learning Skills

| | | | |
|---|---|---|---|
| • | | | |
| • | | | |
| • | | | |
| • | | | |
| • | | | |
| • | | | |
| • | | | |
| • | | | |
| • | | | |
| • | | | |
| • | | | |

# Internet Sites

Use this section to:

- ✓ Find starting places to save you time
- ✓ Gather excellent curriculum oriented Internet sites

Joanne J. Troutner

# Starting Points

| Learning in Motion | //www.learn.motion.com/lim/links/linkmain |
|---|---|

*A monthly top ten list of education sites hitting all curriculum areas. Archives are available.*

| Busy Teachers' WebSite K – 12 | //www.ceismc.gatech.edu/busyt/ |
|---|---|

*Myriad of superb sites listed by curriculum areas*

| B.J. Pinchbeck's Homework Helper | //school.discovery.com/homeworkhelp/bjpinchbeck/ |
|---|---|

*Great collection of curriculum oriented sties designed by an 13 year old & Dad*

| Scout Report for Social Sciences | //scout.cs.wisc.edu/report/socsci/index.html |
|---|---|

*A bi-weekly publication of web sites for researchers and educators.*

| Scout Report for Business & Economics | //scout.cs.wisc.edu/report/bus-econ/index.html |
|---|---|

*A bi-weekly publication of web sites for librarians and content specialists*

| David Levin's Learning@WebSites | //www.ecnet.net/users/gdlevin/home.html |
|---|---|

*Designed for secondary students, categorized by curriculum area, useful for teachers*

| Education Index | //www.educationindex.com/ index.html |
|---|---|

*Good set of reviewed sites with a subject area index*

| Michigan Teacher Network | //mtn.merit.edu |
|---|---|

*Excellent set of teaching links with concise descriptions*

| Education World | //www.education-world.com |
|---|---|

*A searchable database of over 56,000 sites useful in teaching*

| Kathy Schrock's Guide for Educators | //school.discovery.com/schrockguide |
|---|---|

*One of the top lists of sites useful to eductors*

| **Blue Web'n** | //www.kn.pacbell.com/wired/ bluewebn/ |
|---|---|

*Superb sites selected and reviewed by the educational team working on the PacBell Education First Initiative*

| **Curriculum and Instruction** | //www.middleweb.com/ContntCurr.html |
|---|---|

*High quality curriculum and teaching strategies links*

| **The Internet Public Library** | //www.ipl.org/ |
|---|---|

*A great all purpose reference tool with links to most sources you could ever want!*

| **High School Hub** | //highschoolhub.org |
|---|---|

*Free portal to a number of curriculum and high interest sites*

| **Virtual Library Museum Pages** | //www.icom.org/vlmp/ |
|---|---|

*Most comprehensive listing of on-line museums available*

| **Museums on the Web** | //curry.edschool.virginia.edu/it/projects/ Museums/Teacher_Guide/Hotlist/ home.html |
|---|---|

*Subject area access to on-line museums, not at as comprehensive as the Virtual Library pages*

| **Smithsonian Institution** | //www.si.edu/ |
|---|---|

*Subject access to the overwhelming amount of information available at the Smithsonian web sites*

| **Expo Ticket Center** | //www.ibiblio.org/expo/ ticket_office.html |
|---|---|

*Well crafted virtual visit to a number of museums*

| **Encarta Schoolhouse** | //encarta.msn.com/guide/ newschoolhouse.asp |
|---|---|

*Excellent source of class project ideas and topic approaches to using the encyclopedia. Look at the units on the Civil War and the Olympics.*

| **CNN Interactive** | //www.cnn.com// |
|---|---|

*Complete CNN news site with audio and video clips—updated throughout the day*

| **Education Version of CNN** | //fyi.cnn.com/fyi/teachers/ |
|---|---|

*Teacher's edition for using CNN—lesson plans & activities*

| **USA Today** | //www.usatoday.com/ |
|---|---|

*Complete USA Today site updated throughout the day—excellent educational links and lesson plans*

| **PBS** | //www.pbs.org/ |
|---|---|

*Well organized site with information from various PBS programs—good source of beginning Internet information*

| **National Public Radio** | //www.npr.org/ |
|---|---|

*Easy access to sound files from current and past broadcasts—requires audio capabilities*

| **Time Magazine** | //www.time.com/time/ |
|---|---|

*Site contains not only magazine information but Time news information*

| **Newsweek** | //www.msnbc.com/news/NW-front_Front.asp |
|---|---|

*Site contains most of the magazine information*

| **US News & World Report** | //www.usnews.com/usnews/ home.htm |
|---|---|

*Wonderful web site of almost the complete magazine*

| **NY Times Learning Network** | //www.nytimes.com/learning/ |
|---|---|

*Excellent teaching materials designed for use with the print and web version of this newspaper*

| **ThinkQuest Projects** | //www.thinkquest.org/ |
|---|---|

*Access the library of student projects to find wonderful Internet activities*

---

What sites can you add to this list?

Which of these sites will you put to use this week or next?

What unit are you teaching yet this grading period where one or more of these sites will be useful?

# Professional Resources

| ★ **Standards at McREL** | //www.mcrel.org/topics/ |
|---|---|

*A well developed list of articles and questions about the national and state standards movement—select the Standards link*

| ★ **Information Literacy Standards** | //www.ala.org/aasl/ip_nine.html |
|---|---|

*American Association of School Librarians (AASL) standards on information literacy*

| ★ **From Now On** | //www.fno.org/ |
|---|---|

*Thought provoking electronic journal by a former superintendent and director of technology & media*

| ★ **PBS Teacher Connex** | //www.pbs.org/teachersource |
|---|---|

*Internet tutorials, teaching tips, lesson plans, and many other resources*

| ★ **Integrating the Internet** | //l2l.org/pd/ |
|---|---|

*Great set of professional development materials on the Internet and other technology*

| ★ **Using Technology in a Social Studies Classroom** | //www.techlearning.com/db_area/archives/WCE/archives/hutchin.htm |
|---|---|

*One teacher's view of using a number of technologies in a high school classroom*

| ★ ***Education Week*** | //www.edweek.org/ |
|---|---|

*Keep up-to-date with the latest in the profession as well as get school reform information*

| ★ ***National Council for the Social Studies*** | //www.socialstudies.org/ |
|---|---|

*Check the links for notable books, standards, and professional development*

| ★ **New York Times Education Section** | //www.nytimes.com/pages/education/index.html |
|---|---|

*Good place to keep up with the current news of our profession*

| ★ **Hot Topics** | //www.teachersfirst.com/hot.htm |
|---|---|

*Great list of current topics for teachers and for teaching resources*

# Humanities Sites

| ➢ **World Wide Arts Resources** | //wwar.com/ |
|---|---|

*Links to hundreds of museums and galleries*

| ➢ **Fine Arts Museums of San Francisco** | //www.thinker.org/ |
|---|---|

*Keyword searching access to the digitized works in these San Francisco musuems—a real treasuretrove of materials*

| ➢ **National Museum of American Art** | //nmaa-ryder.si.edu/ |
|---|---|

*On-line exhibits and museum information*

| ➢ **National Museum of African Art** | //www.nmafa.si.edu/ |
|---|---|

*A number of on-line exhibits*

| ➢ **Web Museum, Paris** | //www.ibiblio.org/wm/paint/ |
|---|---|

*Medieval art which can only be viewed on the web*

| ➢ **The Louvre** | //www.paris.org/Musees/Louvre/ |
|---|---|

*An English version of numerous images and exhibits*

| ➢ **ArtsEd Net** | //www.getty.edu/artsednet/ |
|---|---|

*Wealth of arts education information and links*

| ➢ **Artsedge** | //artsedge.kennedy-center.org/ |
|---|---|

*Curriculum ideas, professional development, and more*

| ➢ **Music Education Online** | //www.childrensmusicworkshop.com/ |
|---|---|

*Excellent set of links for music educators*

| ➢ **K - 12 Resources for Music Educators** | //www.isd77.k12.mn.us/resources/staffpages/shirk/k12.music.html |
|---|---|

*Wonder set of links*

| ➢ **J.S. Bach Homepage** | //www.jsbach.org/ |
|---|---|

*Excellent set of resources*

| ➢ **Gilbert & Sullivan** | //math.boisestate.edu/gas/index.html |
|---|---|

*Rich archive of works and background*

| ➢ **Playbill On-Line** | //www.playbill.com/ |
|---|---|

*Key to plays on Broadway, London, and other venues*

| ➢ **Ansel Adams** | //www.cdlib.org/adams.html |
|---|---|

*Excellent exhibit of the master's black & white photographs*

| ➢ **Smithsonian Photographs Online** | //photo2.si.edu/index.html |
|---|---|

*Many topics and photos. Excellent resource for interdisciplinary work*

| ➢ **Classical Music Pages** | //w3.rz-berlin.mpg.de/cmp/ classmus.html |
|---|---|

*Excellent collection of resources categorized by time period, music type, or composer name*

| ➢ **Art for Sale** | //www.itdc.sbcss.k12.ca.us/ curriculum/artforsale.html |
|---|---|

*Wonderful lesson plan where students take on the role of professionals in an art brokerage firm*

| ➢ **Classical Net** | //www.classical.net/music/rep/lists/ index.html |
|---|---|

*A quick reference of a vast array of composers*

| ➢ **Instrument Encyclopedia** | //www.si.umich.edu/chico/ instrument/ |
|---|---|

*A quick reference of a vast array of composers*

| ➢ **Dance Dictionary** | //www.arthurmurray.com/htmlws/ dancdict.htm |
|---|---|

*Concise information on a vast number of dance steps*

# English/Language Arts Sites

|  |  |
|---|---|
| **Author Webliography** | //www.lib.lsu.edu/hum/authors.html |

*Good starting point for finding author web sites*

|  |  |
|---|---|
| **Common Errors in English** | //www.wsu.edu/~brians/errors/index.html |

*Concise descriptions and explanations of speaking and writing errors*

|  |  |
|---|---|
| **The Encyclopedia Mythica** | //www.pantheon.org/mythica.html |

*Learn about Greek, Roman, Chinese, Norse, and many other mythologies*

|  |  |
|---|---|
| **The Blue Book of Grammar** | //www.grammarbook.com/ |

*Quick, well indexed set of grammar tools*

|  |  |
|---|---|
| **Visit the Bard** | //www.it.usyd.edu.au/~matty/Shakespeare/ |

*Searchable site with the complete works of Shakespeare*

|  |  |
|---|---|
| **Shakespeare Magazine** | //www.shakespearemag.com/ |

*Be sure to check out the lesson plans link*

|  |  |
|---|---|
| **Atlantic Monthly Poetry** | //www.theatlantic.com/unbound/poetry/poetry.htm |

*Access to the superb poetry published in this magazine*

|  |  |
|---|---|
| **Cyberguides for Literature** | //www.sdcoe.k12.ca.us/score/cyberguide.html |

*A variety of supplementary units based on core literary works*

|  |  |
|---|---|
| **The Camelot Project** | //www.lib.rochester.edu/camelot/cphome.stm |

*Wonderful site chocked full of texts, Arthurian lore, images, and bibliographies*

|  |  |
|---|---|
| **The English Server** | //eserver.org/poetry/ |

*Organized alphabetically by author, an extensive collection of famous poets and their works*

| ✐ **Online Literary Criticism Collection** | //www.ipl.org/ref/litcrit/ |
|---|---|

*Contains 1,253 or more critical websites*

| ✐ **Teacher Guide** | //cagle.slate.msn.com/teacher/ |
|---|---|

*Teacher's guide for using the Professional Cartoonists Index and editorial cartoons in the classroom*

| ✐ **Folklore, Myth, and Legend** | //www.acs.ucalgary.ca/~dkbrown/storfolk.html |
|---|---|

*Great set of links to any number of fairy tales, folklore, and mythology works*

| ✐ **Academy of American Poets** | //www.poets.org/index.cfm |
|---|---|

*Use the search option to find information on over 200 poets*

| ✐ **National Press Club Homepage** | //npc.press.org |
|---|---|

*Links to many news sources which help journalism students*

| ✐ **Purdue Writing Lab Online** | //owl.english.purdue.edu/handouts/index2.html |
|---|---|

*Excellent set of short handouts on numerous writing problems*

| ✐ **Vocabulary** | //www.vocabulary.com |
|---|---|

*A wide range of puzzles and activities to help with vocabulary building*

| ✐ **Bartlett's Familiar Quotations** | //www.bartleby.com/100/ |
|---|---|

*The on-line version of this reference tool*

| ✐ **Visual Thesaurus** | //www.visualthesaurus.com/ |
|---|---|

*A wonderful Java based on-line thesaurus*

| ✐ **Guide to Grammar and Writing** | //ccc.commnet.edu/grammar/index.htm |
|---|---|

*Great handouts plus 77 on-line quizzes*

| ✐ **Researcherpaper.com** | //www.researchpaper.com/ |
|---|---|

*A good set of helpful tools—not a site to download already prepared papers*

| ✐ **A.Word.A.Day** | //www.wordsmith.org/awad/ |
|---|---|

*Subscribe to the e-mail service, which provides you with a wealth of vocabulary building activities or go to the archives*

# WWW Math Sites

| ♦ **Math Resources** | //www.utm.edu/~cesme/math-activities.html |
|---|---|

*Wonderful collection of links to lessons plans and teaching ideas for K – 8 students*

| ♦ **Math Forum** | //forum.swarthmore.edu/ |
|---|---|

*Curriculum resources, discussion of issues, excellent collection of links*

| ♦ **Mathematics—Integrated Units for Grades 5 - 8** | //www.ncsa.uiuc.edu/Edu/RSE/ RSEorange/buttons.html |
|---|---|

*Thought provoking and interesting collection of lesson ideas and information*

| ♦ **Math Baseball** | //www.funbrain.com/math/index.html |
|---|---|

*Fun game based on math skills for one or two players—practice addition, subtraction, multiplication, or division at three skill levels*

| ♦ **How Far Is It?** | //www.escapeartist.com/travel/ howfar.htm |
|---|---|

*Calculates distances, provides longitude, latitude, compass directions*

| ♦ **The Dance of Chance** | //polymer.bu.edu/museum/ |
|---|---|

*Learn about math patterns and fractals in everyday life*

| ♦ **Harcourt School Math Site** | //www.harcourtschool.com/menus/ math_advantage.html |
|---|---|

*Nice set of activities designed to fit with a math textbook and usable for any number of teaching options*

| ♦ **What Good is Math?** | //oncampus.richmond.edu/academics/as/ education/projects/webunits/math/ home.htm |
|---|---|

*Delightful set of activities which illustrate real life uses of math for students*

| ♦ **Fractal Microscope** | //www.ncsa.uiuc.edu/Edu/Fractal/ Fractal_Home.html |
|---|---|

*Enjoy the art and science of mathematics*

| ♦ **Math Lessons** | //www.math.rice.edu/~lanius/Lessons/ |
|---|---|

*A treasuretrove of lesson plan ideas for using the Internet*

| ♦ **Synergetics on the Web** | //www.grunch.net/synergetics/ |
|---|---|

*Excellent resource with complete explanations, history, and many visuals*

| ♦ **Measure 4 Measure** | //www.wolinskyweb.com/measure.htm |
|---|---|

*Chock full of interactive sites which deal with any number of calculations*

| ♦ **The Fibonnacci Numbers** | //www.mcs.surrey.ac.uk/Personal/R.Knott /Fibonacci/fibnat.html |
|---|---|

*Excellent interpretation of the Fibonacci numbers*

| ♦ **World of Escher** | //www.WorldOfEscher.com/ |
|---|---|

*See many tesselations and find out more about the artist*

| ♦ **The National Budget Simulation** | //www.budgetsim.org/nbs/ |
|---|---|

*Try the short version first—good interdisciplinary tool*

| ♦ **Mega Math** | //www.c3.lanl.gov/mega-math/index.html |
|---|---|

*Get the big picture behind a number of math problems and concepts along with ties to the NCTM standards*

| ♦ **Statistics Every Writer Should Know** | //nilesonline.com/stats/ |
|---|---|

*Concise, easy-to-understand explanation of statistics*

| ♦ **Mathematics of Cartography** | //math.rice.edu/~lanius/pres/map/ |
|---|---|

Learn about the making of maps and the wealth of math used to accomplish this

| ♦ **Revisewise Math** | //www.bbc.co.uk/schools/revisewise/ maths/ |
|---|---|

*A number of interactive activities on various math topics*

| ♦ **Virtual Manipulatives** | //matti.usu.edu/nlvm/nav/vlibrary.html |
|---|---|

*A wide range of options for preschool through grade 12*

Joanne J. Troutner

# WWW Science Sites

| ✓ **Access Excellence Resource Center** | //www.accessexcellence.org/RC/ |
|---|---|

*Good jumping off point for science educators*

| ✓ **The Exploratorium Homepage** | //www.exploratorium.edu/ |
|---|---|

*Exciting on-line exhibits*

| ✓ **The Heart** | //sln.fi.edu/biosci/heart.html |
|---|---|

*Wonderful interactive simulation*

| ✓ **The Interactive Frog Dissection** | //curry.edschool.Virginia.EDU/go/frog |
|---|---|

*Almost like real life and saves an animal*

| ✓ **University of California Museum of Paleontology** | //www.ucmp.berkeley.edu/ |
|---|---|

*Superb on-line exhibits and history section*

| ✓ **The Visible Human Project** | //www.nlm.nih.gov/research/visible/visible_human.html |
|---|---|

*Complete anatomically detailed, 3D representations of female and male humans*

| ✓ **Rainforest Virtual Tour** | //www.bsrsi.msu.edu/rfrc/tour/rainforest.html |
|---|---|

*Nicaragua and the rainforest*

| ✓ **NASA** | //www.nasa.gov/ |
|---|---|

*Overall entry to the massive amount of NASA information*

| ✓ **Views of the Solar System** | //www.solarviews.com/eng/homepage.htm |
|---|---|

*Over 950 images and 880 MB of information*

| ✓ **Science Learning Network** | //www.sln.org/ |
|---|---|

*A wealth of inquiry oriented science activities developed by various museums*

| ✓ **Chemistry Teaching Resources** | //www.anachem.umu.se/eks/pointers.htm |
|---|---|

*Extensive, well organized set of links for chemistry teachers*

| ✓ **Space Image Libraries** | //www.okstate.edu/aesp/ image.html |
|---|---|

*A variety of sources presented by NASA's Aerospace Education Services Program*

| ✓ **The Why Files—Science Behind the News** | //whyfiles.org/index.html |
|---|---|

*Funded by NSF, a delightful collection of scientific information*

| ✓ **JASON Project** | //www.jasonproject.org/ |
|---|---|

*Entry to the variety of materials generated by this project*

| ✓ **Tornado Project** | //www.tornadoproject.com/ |
|---|---|

*Excellent pictures, current information, and myths*

| ✓ **Volcano World** | //volcano.und.nodak.edu/ |
|---|---|

Ask a volcanolgist a question and gather myriad information

| ✓ **Earthquake** | //quake.wr.usgs.gov/ |
|---|---|

*Latest information about seismic activity in the US*

| ✓ **Worldwide Earthquake Information** | //www.civeng.carleton.ca/ cgi-bin/quakes/ |
|---|---|

*Global information and links to maps*

| ✓ **The International Symposium on Environmental Issues—Sydney, Australia** | //www.itdc.sbcss.k12.ca.us/ curriculum/ozone.html |
|---|---|

*Excellent WebQuest where students learn about ozone, pollution, and the environment*

| ✓ **bioSURF** | //www.phschool.com/science/ biosurf/ |
|---|---|

*Good example of an Internet site tied to a textbook, Addison Wesley's Biology*

| ✓ **Cells Alive** | //www.cellsalive.com/ |
|---|---|

*Wonderful videos about viruses, bacterium, parasites, and blood cells*

| ✓ **Ocean Planet Online** | //seawifs.gsfc.nasa.gov/ ocean_planet.html |
|---|---|

*Wonderful Smithsonian exhibit with environmental information as well*

# Social Studies Sites

| ★ **The History Net** | //www.historynet.com// |
|---|---|

*Extensive, easy-to-use site of American and World history, which includes primary source material*

| ★ **The History Place** | //www.historyplace.com/ |
|---|---|

*Wonderful site filled with photos, materials, and special exhibits*

| ★ **Exploring Ancient World Cultures** | //eawc.evansville.edu/index.htm |
|---|---|

*A selective, introductory look at various Internet resources on ancient cultures*

| ★ **CNN Black History Month Page** | //www.cnn.com/EVENTS/black_history/index.html |
|---|---|

*Compilation of materials from February 1996 and a wonderful set of links to related sites*

| ★ **InSite—Canada's Digital Collections** | //collections.ic.gc.ca/ |
|---|---|

*Excellent set of subject based collections of digital images relating to Canadian history and culture*

| ★ **The History Channel** | //www.historychannel.com/ |
|---|---|

*Superb companion to the television History Channel*

| ★ **Internet Medieval Sourcebook** | //www.fordham.edu/halsall/sbook.html |
|---|---|

*Excellent source of teaching materials for this time period*

| ★ **BBC—History** | //www.bbc.co.uk/history/ |
|---|---|

*A wide range of topics from a British point of view.*

| ★ **National Geographic** | //www.nationalgeographic.com/ |
|---|---|

*An electronic version of the classic publication plus links to Traveler magazine and a superb map machine*

| ★ **Online Courts for Kids** | //access.wa.gov/kids/courts.asp |
|---|---|

*Learn about law by surfing the web—a superb collection of resources*

| ★ **Popular Songs in American History** | //www.contemplator.com/america/ |
|---|---|

*Historical background plus the music files to actually play the songs—ranges from17th century to mid 1900's*

| ★ **Museum of Financial History** | //www.financialhistory.org/ |
|---|---|

*See the impact the economy and finances had throughout history*

| ★ **Links to the Past** | //www.cr.nps.gov/ |
|---|---|

*Use the US National Park System to find historical information*

| ★ **You Be the Historian** | //www.americanhistory.si.edu/hohr/springer/index.htm |
|---|---|

*Wonderful simulation for students*

| ★ **Eyewitness: History Through the Eyes of Those Who Lived It** | //www.ibiscom.com/index.html |
|---|---|

*Excellent set of materials with primary source information*

| ★ **Time 100** | //www.time.com/time/time100/ |
|---|---|

*Explore the top 20 people in five areas of the past century*

| ★ **Ancient Egypt** | //www.ancientegypt.co.uk/I |
|---|---|

*Virtual exhibit from the British Museum*

| ★ **The Victorian Web** | //www.victorianweb.org/ |
|---|---|

*Wonderful set of resource for the study of the Victorian era*

| ★ **Loyalty or Liberty?** | //www.history.org/history/teaching/revolution/loyalty.html |
|---|---|

*Work through a simulation about deciding to stay on the plantation or take actions to become free*

| ★ **Picturing the Century** | //www.archives.gov/exhibit_hall/picturing_the_century/swf/flash_intro.html |
|---|---|

*Collections of photographs from well known photographers plus a number of theme related galleries*

| ★ **The First Ladies** | //www.whitehouse.gov/history/firstladies/I |
|---|---|

*Explore the contributions of the President's wives*

# Glossary

*Address*
The characters used to identify and locate a computer, directory, file or person on the Internet. The domain name, (i.e. wvec.k12.in.us), is the address for an Internet server. An e-mail address includes the person or organization's name, ( i.e. snugs@wvec.k12.in.us).

*ARPAnet*
The Advanced Research projects Agency network, which is the predecessor of the Internet. It was funded by the US Department of Defense.

*AUP*
Acceptable Use Policy. A document which explains the rules of Internet use and approved actions. Upon signing the Internet user agrees to abide by the rules and policies.

*Bandwidth*
As it refers to the Internet, the amount of data which can be transmitted per second from one computer to another over a phone line or other Internet connection.

*Bookmark*
A tool available in most web browsers for storing commonly used addresses for easy access. A wonderful feature for helping keep students on track when using the Internet. Can be exported to disk and then reloaded for later use. Same as *My Favorites* with Internet Explorer.

*Browser*
Commonly referred to as "web browser", this is the software which allows the user to navigate easily around the Internet and look at WWW sites. Common browsers are Netscape and Internet Explorer.

*Domain name*
The address of a computer written in letters instead of the IP address, which is in numbers. The top level domain is the fair right set of letters —.com, .edu, .org, .gov, etc. identifies companies, educational institutions, organizations, government entities. The mid-level domain identifies the specific organization. For instance, the West Central Indiana Community Network uses the domain name wcic.org.

*Download*
The transferring of a file over a telecommunications link, usually from an Internet server to your own computer. Uploading is the reverse process of sending a file from your computer to an Internet server or another computer.

*E-mail*
Electronic mail. Sending and receiving messages over the Internet or any other telecommunications systems such as AOL or others.

*FAQ*
Frequently Asked Questions. Several WWW sites and other places on the Internet provide files which contain answers to often asked questions. A good source of information for beginners.

*Filter*
Software or hardware which allows the user to restrict access to certain sites on the Internet.

*Flame*
Writing an angry and inflammatory message to someone via e-mail. This term also refers to the message. This practice is not considered good netiquette.

*Freeware*
The author of this type of software allows users to copy and distribute the software at no charge.

*GIF*
Graphics Interchange Format. A graphics format that can be used on several computer platforms. GIF files usually end with a .gif.

*Gopher*
Developed by the University of Minnesota, this is a text-based system used for accessing information on the Internet. It does not require the use of a web browser.

*Home Page*
This is the first page one sees when visiting a World Wide Web site.

*Hotlist*
The same as a bookmark list, a set of commonly visited sites. Both are features of most web browsers.

*HTML*
Hypertext Markup Language. This is the programming language used to develop World Wide Web sites.

*HTTP*
HyperText Transfer Protocol. This is the electronics communication method used by the World Wide Web.

*Internet*
The global network of networks that connects millions of computers called hosts.

*ISP*
Internet Service Provider. An organization or commercial entity that provides access to the Internet.

*Internet Site*
A computer host containing information which is connected to the Internet.

*IP Address*
Internet Protocol Number. A unique numerical address assigned to each computer on the Internet. The series of four numbers (i.e. 251.345. 25.126) is translated into the domain name.

*JPEG*
A compressed graphics format designed for transmitting photographs. JPEG files normally end in .jpg, .jpeg, or .jpe.

*Mirror Site*
An Internet server which contains a complete copy of the files on a second Internet server. This tool is used for sites which handle a large number of hits or traffic.

*Netiquette*
The rules of conduct or etiquette for the using the Internet. Violation of these policies can result the ISP's canceling an offender's Internet access.

*Search Engine*
A computer program which scans the Internet for information matching the search terms it is given. Search engines can search the world wide web, newsgroups, and other Internet sources.

*URL*
Universal Resource Locator. The method used to locate a specific resource on the Internet. Also referred to as the location's address.

*World Wide Web*
This is an Internet browsing system which allows point and click navigation. Technically, the family of connected Internet sites which can be reached using HyperText Transfer Protocol or HTTP.

## ABOUT THE AUTHOR

**Joanne Troutner** is an experienced classroom teacher and district administrator as well as an outstanding author. She has been a library media specialist for grades K – 12, a $7^{th}$ and $8^{th}$ grade English teacher, and a district technology/media director. Joanne writes a regular Internet Resource column for an international magazine, *Teacher Librarian*, as well as being the Web Site Columnist for *Booklist*. Joanne is the author of *The Media Specialist*, *The Microcomputer*, and *The Curriculum*, a pioneering work in the area of technology. She gives Internet and other technology presentations at local, state, regional, and national conferences. Joanne also has served on the United States Department of Education Telecommunications Task Force and as a grant reviewer for the US Department of Education.

www.ingramcontent.com/pod-product-compliance
Ingram Content Group UK Ltd.
Pitfield, Milton Keynes, MK11 3LW, UK
UKHW061831190726
13855UKWH00005B/1747